cling

cling

Choosing a Lifestyle of
Intimacy with God

KIM CASH TATE

Discovery House.
from Our Daily Bread Ministries

Cling: Choosing a Lifestyle of Intimacy with God

Discovery House is affiliated with Our Daily Bread Ministries, Grand Rapids, Michigan.

Requests for permission to quote from this book should be directed to: Permissions Department, Discovery House, P.O. Box 3566, Grand Rapids, MI 49501, or contact us by e-mail at permissionsdept@dhp.org.

ISBN: 978-1-62707-595-4

Printed in the United States of America
First printing in 2017

Contents

Introduction

Invitation to Intimacy

It had been a very difficult twenty-four hours. I'd been blindsided by something—a very hard something—that one of our teens was going through. My husband and I met in this child's room with questions—but with little forthcoming in reply, there were more questions. And confusion. And fear.

Through the night, anxious thoughts pinged from one corner of my mind to the other, the ache of my heart palpable. There's nothing like the pain of knowing your child's pain—and knowing there's nothing you can do to fix it. I'm a weird emotional mix . . . a deep feeler, not a big crier. So that night I did a lot of feeling. The next morning, I was surprised when not only tears but *sobs* showed up. While driving. On the highway.

Shaking, hands swiping like wiper blades, it became apparent that the sobs were reaching back—to the last heartache, and the one before that. And disappointments and difficulties. So much, it seemed, just in the past two years, all of it banding together at that moment and hurtling me toward despair.

"Lord, why? Just *why?*" I spoke aloud, my words and the ugly cry echoing to the back seat of my minivan. "What is going *on?* I don't get why there's one thing after another—and it *hurts.*"

On and on I went, fumbling for tissues at sixty miles per hour, when, about two exits from home, I realized . . . I'd been having a rolling conversation with God since the night before.

As we sat in our teen's room: *Lord, please give us the words. Please give us the wisdom. Help us, Lord, to understand. Show us what to do.*

As I drifted in and out of sleep that night: *Lord, we need You. My child needs You. Please protect and strengthen. Please uphold by Your right hand. We can't fix this situation, but You can.*

When I woke up: *Lord, I feel like I'm in a fog. I don't know what to think or feel . . .*

As I made breakfast, with worship music filling my earbuds: *I praise You, Lord. You are sovereign. You are faithful. There is nothing too hard for You.*

In the car: *Lord, this is too hard!*

And it hit me—I'm *always* talking to Him. I talk to my husband, of course, and to my kids and other people, but to God far more than anyone else, because He's always with me. I send up heart reactions, mental musings, complaints, anxieties, questions—*what should I cook for dinner? why am I so moody today?*—as well as praise. How could you not when the sky puts on a show at sunset?

Fresh tears fell—different tears, joy-in-the-midst tears—as I understood *why* this realization was hitting me. It was the Lord, revealing what I hadn't fully grasped, the thing that would halt the despair—He had become my for-real *Friend.*

And that soul level connection had come from clinging.

It became a prayer years ago: "Lord, help me to *cling* to You." I had been enamored with the word, struck by it during a study of

Deuteronomy. In that book, Moses gave final instructions to the people of Israel before they entered into the Promised Land of Canaan.

It had been quite a journey to get to that point. Centuries before, as recorded in Genesis, God had sworn to Abraham, Isaac, and Jacob that He would give their descendants this land. Only a few generations later, though, those descendants were being held captive in Egypt—and Pharaoh had no intention of letting them go.

But problems for humanity are opportunities for God to demonstrate His power. And He did so, through plague after plague He sent upon the land of Egypt. When Pharaoh still refused to let the Israelites go, God struck down every firstborn in Egypt—every one, that is, except for those of the people of Israel, who were protected by the blood of the lamb over their doorposts. Pharaoh finally relented, telling the people to get out. And they did, that very night.

Imagine the scene—more than six hundred thousand Israelites moving in haste from the land. But they could only move so fast on foot. Before long, Pharaoh changed his mind and sent hundreds of Egyptian chariots after them. The Israelites panicked. Why had Moses taken them from Egypt? Surely they would be better off as slaves than to die in the wilderness! Despite the miracles they had seen God perform in Egypt, their eyes were on the power of the Egyptians.

But it was God who had hardened Pharaoh's heart. It was God who was in control, *still*. And it was God who would once again deliver His people.

The Israelites were camped near the Red Sea, and by anyone's reckoning, trapped. But the Lord made a way *through* the sea, instructing Moses to lift his staff over the water so that it parted. With a wall of water to the right and a wall of water to the left, the Israelites crossed on dry ground. And when the Egyptians pursued, the Lord threw them into confusion. He told Moses to stretch out his hand over the sea once more, causing the waters to return to normal. The entire Egyptian army drowned.

The Israelites were in awe. Can't you imagine them on the shore gaping at one another? "Did we really see what we just saw? Did the sea just . . . *part* like that?" They had been unsure about those chariots at first, frightened in the moment. But this God who had shown up in Egypt—He was the real deal. They feared Him now. They *believed*. Sang songs of rejoicing.

In a few short weeks, the Israelites were comfortably ensconced in the land of milk and honey, enjoying the fruits of the promise.

Well, actually—there were a few more issues along the way. Lots of grumbling. Rebellion. Unbelief. Oh, and this one little incident with worshipping a golden calf . . . It *could* have been a relatively short trip. But because of their unbelief, God pronounced judgment. An entire generation would wander and die in the wilderness, never to see the land that was promised.

And so, *forty years later*, it was the children, the next generation, to whom Moses was speaking in Deuteronomy. Finally, the people of Israel were about to enter the Promised Land, but Moses needed to prepare them. He reminded them of the Lord's deliverance from Egypt and from other enemies who had threatened them along the way. He recalled the laws of God, and Israel's rebellion and unbelief in the wilderness. And He looked forward, giving instruction as to how the people should live in the new land, how they were to walk with God.

This is where I was some years ago, during my study of Deuteronomy, when I saw it, that one word:

*"You shall fear the L*ord* your God; you shall serve Him and **cling** to Him, and you shall swear by His name."*

Deuteronomy 10:20

And again:

*"You shall follow the L*ord* your God and fear Him; and you shall keep His commandments, listen to His voice, serve Him, and **cling** to Him."*

Deuteronomy 13:4

no Marriage in heaven
Mark 12:24   Luke 20:34

And I was smitten. There is something about that word—it's different from the other verbs in those verses. When it comes to our relationship with an almighty, holy God, we expect that we should fear Him, keep His commandments, and listen to His voice. It's no surprise that we must follow and serve Him.

But *cling* to Him?

The other commands can be satisfied from a certain distance. I can even follow from a distance, as long as I'm headed in the same direction. But clinging puts me in God's face, smack up against His person. *Glued* to Him. It's personal. Intimate.

The word itself is *dabaq* in the Hebrew. It means "cling," "cleave," or "keep close." Your Bible translation might render it "hold fast," or something similar. The same Hebrew word is found in Genesis 2:24—"Therefore shall a man leave his father and his mother, and shall **cleave** unto his wife: and they shall be one flesh" (KJV). It's no small thing that this "cleaving" and becoming "one flesh" is also an illustration of Jesus and His church (Ephesians 5:31–32).

It doesn't get more intimate than clinging. We were created to cling to God. Our souls thrive in that place. Without it, we languish. We crave it, though we often don't even know what it is we're craving.

I was in that place. For the longest time, I didn't know why I was so drawn to the word *cling* and all that it suggested. I didn't realize how much I craved deep intimacy, a feeling that went back to my early childhood.

It's one of my most vivid memories as a girl: sitting on the edge of the twin bed, my face angled toward the window, eyes peeled for my daddy. I'd be excited about our planned outing, but mostly I just wanted to see him. I loved being around my daddy. We had fun, laughed a lot. And when he said he was coming, I couldn't keep away from that window . . . even as daylight turned to dusk. And dusk turned to night. It was only then, after my mom tried several times to coax me away from the window, that I'd finally relent.

He wasn't coming. Again.

I don't hold it against my dad. To this day, we have a great relationship. Still laugh a lot. But for a season after my parents' divorce—when I was four—he'd make promises he couldn't keep. And my little-girl mind thought more than once, *I must not really matter. He must not love me.*

Because there was no intimacy. There was no *cling*, in the sense of a felt closeness.

As I got older, I tried to fill that void. It was never a conscious thing, but looking back, something in me wanted to cling. I wanted to feel special to someone. I wanted to matter. That's what enticed me about sex—the intimacy it would bring. Or so I thought. It led me to cling in ways I shouldn't have, leaving my soul an even more fractured mess.

So when Bill Tate walked into my life, this soul-wrecked girl, given my history, was skeptical at first—but soon thankful. I was twenty-three at the time, twenty-six when we married. More than two decades later, I know this husband of mine was a gift. He's the only man who has ever committed himself fully to me. The only man who has loved me and been there for me consistently. The only man who time and again has let me know how much I matter.

But let's be honest. Those of us who've been married any length of time know that our spouses can't be all things to us. They can't heal our every hurt, can't fill our every void. As much of a gift as Bill was, I needed more than Bill.

And the Lord graciously delivered. A year into our marriage, the same God who rescued the Israelites from Egypt rescued me from darkness and brought me to Himself. I didn't know that I'd been chosen before the foundation of the world. Didn't know I was loved with an everlasting love. I didn't know that every time I sat on that twin bed with tears in my eyes, wondering if my father cared, there was a Father in heaven who desired to have a relationship with me—who would invite me to *cling* to Him.

That's how I see "clinging to God"—not so much of a command as a gracious invitation.

Maybe, like me, you had earthly relationships that left you wanting. Or maybe those relationships were everything God intended. No matter where we sit on that spectrum, there is a place—deep in each of our souls—reserved for God alone. A place only He knows and understands. A place only He can reach. It's where you are healed, nurtured, and comforted. It's where you weep and nestle in His arms. It's where the two of you vibe and share. It's where you dance to a glorious rhythm, no matter the circumstances. This was God's will for us from the foundation of the world: that we would dwell closely with Him.

That's what this book is about—choosing a lifestyle of intimacy with God. But how do we *do* that? "Intimacy with God" can seem like such a foreign concept. And "clinging"? How do we do *that?*

In this book, we will explore intimacy with God from various angles. We'll consider the ways in which God has already been moving toward us to establish intimacy; how we can cultivate a lifestyle of intimacy with God in tangible, everyday ways; how God uses trials and suffering in our lives to draw us near; and even how we sometimes drive wedges between ourselves and God.

Are you up for some real talk? I hope so, because I want to be real about even the immoral clinging we may have done in the past, and how we can be healed. Throughout, we will examine the lives of actual people from the pages of Scripture who chose (or didn't choose) to cling to God.

Clinging to God is the source of ultimate blessing and protection, of inexplicable joy and peace. Within His embrace is a place we can be strong and courageous in the Lord—because we *know* He is with us and we are with Him. But in choosing a lifestyle of intimacy with God, we must first be in a true relationship with God. We'll take a look at that first, traveling as far back as the beginning of human history, to see how humankind went from clinging to God to being separated from God, then having the gracious opportunity to once again . . . cling.

1

Created to Cling

I often wonder what life was like in the Garden of Eden. In particular, I wonder what *life with God* was like in its perfect state. I'd love a "day in the life" account in early Genesis, detailing the dynamics of Adam and Eve's interaction with the Lord. Even with the accounts we are given, my curiosity abounds.

For example, when God "brought [every beast and bird] to the man to see what he would call them" (Genesis 2:19), how did Adam experience that? Surely he knew he was in the presence of Almighty God, though the Bible says that since God the Father "is spirit" (John 4:24), "no one has seen God at any time" (John 1:18). But there they were together, Adam naming the living creatures. Was he speaking aloud to God? Did Adam hear an audible response? Any good-natured laughter over his choices?

And after God put Adam to sleep and fashioned Eve from one of his ribs, the Lord "brought her to the man" (Genesis 2:22). What an image that sparks in my mind. What was it like for Eve, that first walk down the aisle? Were any words exchanged with her Lord, her very Creator, as He presented her as a bride to her husband?

Though my curiosity is high—and I look forward to learning more in glory—I'm thankful for the deep insight the book of Genesis already gives. Interestingly, it was written by Moses after the Israelites' exodus from Egypt. This nation of people had been delivered from slavery by God—but all they had known was Egyptian rule and Egyptian gods, which were many. As God's chosen people, the Israelites needed to know who *He* was. They needed to know His power and authority. They needed to know Him as Creator. And they needed to know that they were created for relationship with God.

Imagine Moses, by the Spirit of God, imparting the creation account for the first time. How fascinating to hear of God at work, in total command. The verbs alone throughout the first chapter of Genesis speak to His power and sovereignty:

"God created . . ."
"God said . . ."
"God separated . . ."
"God called . . ."
"God made . . ."
"God placed . . ."
"God blessed . . ."

And how telling to hear that God not only created with power but with purpose—an expanse (heaven) to separate the waters below from the waters above; the sun and moon to separate day from night and for signs and seasons; plants and trees with seed to bear fruit after their kind; creatures designed for the sea, birds to fly in the open expanse, and beasts, cattle, and creeping things for the earth.

All of this was good in God's eyes, but He hadn't yet reached the apex. He had purposed much more.

God Gets Personal

On the sixth day of creation, God said, "Let Us make man in Our image, according to Our likeness" (Genesis 1:26). What an amazing turn in the creation account—I can just see Moses's listeners coming to full attention. Thus far, the account had been rather impersonal.

"Let there be light."

"Let there be an expanse . . ."

"Let the earth sprout vegetation . . ."

"Let the earth bring forth living creatures . . ."

God was fully involved in creating, but the objects were all outside of Himself. They had nothing to do with Him personally. But now, "Let Us . . ."

So much in those words! For the first time, God reveals that He exists in relationship with others. Moses's audience would not have fully understood the "Us," but we have the privilege of living on this side of the cross. I love that both Genesis and the Gospel of John begin with the same three words: "In the beginning." John gives us further enlightenment about that "Us."

In the beginning was the Word, and the Word was with God, and the Word was God. He was in the beginning with God. All things came into being through Him, and apart from Him nothing came into being that has come into being.

John 1:1–3

How stunning that we would be given such rich insight—Jesus, the Word, the Son of God was there in the beginning, creating. Jesus was *with* God, in relationship, together with the Holy Spirit (Genesis 1:2). "Let Us" is a beautiful statement of the divine Godhead.

But perhaps even more stunning is that this divine Trinity would desire to bring others into relationship with itself. As one, the three members of the Trinity would,

". . . make man in Our image, according to Our likeness."

Genesis 1:26

What did this mean? Unlike anything else God made—from the sky and the sea to birds, beasts, and sea creatures—humankind would be unique. We would have higher characteristics, such as the ability to think abstractly, to reason, to feel emotion, to create and to appreciate creation, to know right from wrong and to choose right from wrong. And in addition to the mental and moral aspects of God's image in us, there is this special one: the relational.

With humanity God got personal.

Being made in His image means we can have a relationship with Him. We can talk to Him. We can hear Him. Our minds can know Him. Our hearts can worship Him. We can love and obey Him. When we do these things, we are clinging to Him.

Nothing else in creation was made with "clinging" in mind. This distinction, this ability to walk in close fellowship, was reserved for humankind.

We were created by God to cling to Him.

Adam and Eve enjoyed perfect fellowship with God from the moment they came into existence. Hearing from God, talking with God, walking with God—clinging to God—was their life, sunup to sundown. They knew nothing else.

But things changed. Even before Moses told of this dramatic turn of events, his audience had to know. Something had gone wrong, very wrong. Life was no longer perfect. The people could look around and see nothing but wilderness, not a beautiful garden. And among their great multitude, which of them had known a life of walking with God? Even Moses, adopted as a baby into Pharaoh's family, was upwards of eighty years old when he met God at the burning bush.

How could that be? If God had made humanity uniquely, in His image, and to dwell intimately with Him, why now did He seem so far off? Why did people not *know* Him?

I can identify with those Israelites who were born and raised in Egypt. I spent much of my life distant from the true and living God.

Raised in Prince George's County, Maryland, just outside Washington, D.C., I was blessed with parents who loved me and instilled admirable values. Since both of them had college degrees, education was uppermost. For many years I attended Catholic schools, not for any spiritual guidance they might offer, but for the academics. My path was marked—college, career, and ultimately, financial independence. I stayed true to that path. After graduating from the University of Maryland, I earned a law degree from the George Washington University, clerked for a federal judge in Wisconsin, and worked as a litigation associate at a large Wisconsin law firm. By the age of twenty-seven, I was married, owner of a new home, and on track for promotion to partner. In my mind, I had the makings of success.

But I also had a critical void. The deepest and truest part of me, the part that should have been alive to God, was dead. Mentally, intellectually, even relationally, I was enjoying the fruit of having been made in God's image. But I was missing the sweetest element—knowing Him.

Growing up, I did know *about* Him. Though we weren't churchgoers, at St. Margaret's elementary I learned about Jesus—His goodness, His miracles, His dying on the cross. In fact, I was shaken by the cross. I'll never forget an Easter observance in third grade, when we had the Stations of the Cross during the school day. Our class filed into the sanctuary and began moving from picture to picture, pausing at each image that depicted Jesus on the day of His crucifixion. By the time we got to Jesus hanging on the cross, nails piercing His hands and feet, breath leaving His body, I was in tears. Even the knowledge that He rose again—I never doubted that—didn't comfort me. I couldn't understand: How could something so awful happen to someone so good?

I didn't know Jesus's death had anything to do with me. I didn't know it was *for* me. That little girl staring at the cross didn't know Jesus died so she could have a relationship with Him—so she could cling to Him—and His dying was the only way that that could happen. Because that girl had been born in sin. And being born in sin meant she was separated from God, and owed a sin debt—death (Romans 6:23). Though Jesus was without sin, He willingly died for her, to pay that debt.

But how did we all get here? What happened to that idyllic state where a man and woman were born into relationship with God and dwelled intimately with Him? Why was God now so far off, such that those people of Israel who sat listening to Moses could live most of their lives without knowing Him? Such that you and I could live our lives apart from Him?

The Garden: From Clinging to Separation

You've heard the expression, "It's too good to be true." The implication is that you can't believe some particular thing because *nothing* is that good. But that doesn't apply to the Garden of Eden. It was very good—and it was very true. A perfect setting with perfect people who had a perfect relationship with their Creator. Of course, God was why everything was perfect, because *He* is perfect and true. And there was no expiration date. God created Adam and Eve to live forever, along with their descendants who would "fill the earth" (Genesis 1:28).

But even in that idyllic setting, there was an enemy. He appeared as a serpent to the woman, and that serpent is identified clearly to us in the last book of the Bible: "And the great dragon was thrown down, the serpent of old who is called the devil and Satan, who deceives the whole world" (Revelation 12:9).

Where did this devil come from, the serpent that appeared to the woman way back in the beginning? Thankfully, the Bible gives us a behind-the-scenes glimpse. Stick with me, because we're about to move for a moment to the middle of the Bible, and it may seem like a rabbit trail. But the beauty of Scripture is that it interprets itself: we find nuggets throughout which add layer upon layer of our understanding. And understanding this enemy is critical, not only to comprehend what happened with Adam and Eve but to our own spiritual state. There are two prophets—Ezekiel and Isaiah—who reveal much about this enemy that appeared in the Garden.

First, a passage in Ezekiel focuses on "the leader of Tyre," a city north of Israel. God was bringing judgment on that leader because his heart was lifted up in pride, and he called himself a god (Ezekiel 28:1–2). Then, a few verses later, the focus moves from the leader of Tyre to the spirit behind him. God has a word for the "the *king* of Tyre":

"You had the seal of perfection,
Full of wisdom and perfect in beauty.
You were in Eden, the garden of God;
Every precious stone was your covering:
The ruby, the topaz, and the diamond;
The beryl, the onyx and the jasper;
The lapis lazuli, the turquoise and the emerald;
And the gold, the workmanship of your settings and sockets,
Was in you.
On the day that you were created
They were prepared.
You were the anointed cherub who covers,
And I placed you there."

Ezekiel 28:12–14

From only three verses, we learn telling information about this "king of Tyre." First, clearly, he is not an earthly king. He's a powerful angelic being. Like Adam and Eve, he was created by God and placed by God in the Garden. He was perfect.

So what went wrong? Pride. "Your heart was lifted up because of your beauty" (Ezekiel 28:17). Isaiah tells us more about this being's arrogance:

"But you said in your heart,
'I will ascend to heaven;
I will raise my throne above the stars of God,
And I will sit on the mount of assembly
In the recesses of the north.
I will ascend above the heights of the clouds;

I will make myself like the Most High.'"

Isaiah 14:13–14

It wasn't enough to enjoy the immense goodness God had given— the perfection, the wisdom, the beauty, the stature of being anointed "the cherub who covers." This angelic being wanted more. He wanted to be like God, to supplant God. And all that was good turned corrupt. Once filled with wisdom, he became "internally filled with violence" (Ezekiel 28:16), and was marked by a multitude of iniquities (Ezekiel 28:18).

As a result, he was cast down by God. Instead of bearing the majestic title of "anointed cherub," he is known as Satan (which means "adversary"), the devil, the god of this world, the dragon, and—as we turn back to the Garden in Genesis—the serpent.

Let's picture this. God has created a man and a woman who have perfect intimacy with Him. The hallmark of their existence is *relationship*, and not just the relationship between the two of them—it includes their relationship with God. And there's the devil who has made himself an enemy of God—watching these humans God made, humans who are enjoying His presence.

The enemy didn't want them clinging to God. He had to separate them. And the only thing that could separate God and people was sin.

Of course, the devil came up with a plan. "Now the serpent was more crafty than any beast of the field which the LORD God had made" (Genesis 3:1). He chose which person he would approach (the woman) and the rhetorical device he would use (a question):

"Indeed, has God said, 'You shall not eat from any tree of the garden'?"

One question, loaded. The enemy knew God had not said that. To the contrary, God had given much freedom, saying, "From any tree of the garden you may eat freely" (Genesis 2:16). There was only *one* tree from which they could not eat, the tree of the knowledge of good and evil. If they disobeyed here, they would die. Still, by posing the question, Satan *called into question* what God had said.

"Don't cling to God's word," he may as well have said. "Second-guess it instead."

The woman answered, clarifying that she and Adam could eat from all the trees in the garden except the one in the middle. They couldn't eat from that one—or touch it, she said—or they would die.

God hadn't said anything about touching. The enemy knew that. It was the eating that he wanted.

> *The serpent said to the woman, "You surely will not die! For God knows that in the day you eat from it your eyes will be opened, and you will be like God, knowing good and evil."*
>
> Genesis 3:4–5

You won't cling to God if you regard Him as untrue.

You won't cling to God if you feel you can't trust Him.

You won't cling to God if you question His goodness toward you.

And you won't cling to God if you want to elevate yourself to god-like status.

These were the buttons the enemy pushed to entice the woman to sin—to separate her from her God. Satan himself had wanted to be like God, and saw where it got him—cast down from heaven. If he could get the woman to share the same lust, she would bite . . . and be cast away from God's presence as well.

I can practically see the serpent's eyes glued to her, watching for her next move, wondering if his persuasion worked. Would she do it? Or would she cling to God by resisting the temptation and obeying what God had said?

The woman turned her gaze toward the forbidden tree and fixed her eyes on it, maybe for the first time. And then—

> *When the woman saw that the tree was good for food, and that it was a delight to the eyes, and that the tree was desirable to make one wise, she took from its fruit and ate; and she gave also to her husband with her, and he ate.*
>
> Genesis 3:6

The perfect people and their perfect relationship with God were no more. When God came walking in the garden, instead of welcoming Him, "the man and his wife hid themselves from the presence of the LORD God" (Genesis 3:8).

I have to say that again:

They hid themselves from His presence.

How heartbreaking! Because of sin, they were hiding from God rather than clinging to Him. Sin had broken their fellowship—their intimacy. God had said they would die in the day they ate from the tree, and they did—spiritually and relationally. Dead in their trespasses and sins, their spirits were no longer alive to God (Ephesians 2:1). And rather than live forever, they would one day die a physical death.

Meanwhile, Adam and his wife would live under cursed conditions and be driven from their home: "therefore the LORD God sent him out from the garden of Eden" (Genesis 3:23).

Made in the image of God, made for intimacy with God, humans were now being sent out *by God* from the paradise He'd created for them. God is holy and righteous, and could not abide with sin. But He is also compassionate and loving. I imagine He Himself found it heartbreaking.

And it wasn't just about Adam and Eve. God knew that their bad choice would impact everyone born after them, including you and me. All of humankind would be born with the stain of sin.

2

Re-created to Cling

I 've been feeling like it's wrong, the whole sex-outside-of-marriage thing."

I broached the subject with Bill tentatively, not sure what he'd say, still grappling with my own thoughts. We'd moved to Madison, Wisconsin, a year and a half before to start our careers, and had rented an apartment together, then built a house. We'd never once questioned the morality of it. What's more, we were only four months shy of our planned wedding—our living together shouldn't have mattered at that late stage. But I couldn't shake it. It was bothering me. And I offered the only solution I could think of: maybe we should abstain until our wedding day.

"Well, yeah, if you want to take it to that level, of course it's wrong," said Bill, recalling his Catholic upbringing. "But since when have we cared about that?" He paused. "I hear you, though. Maybe we should abstain. Or better yet, we could get married now, instead of waiting until May."

It seemed ludicrous. Was he suggesting we chuck all of our wedding plans of the past year?

Seeing my face, Bill clarified, "I'm not saying to cancel our May wedding. Just get married early and tell only a few people."

Two weeks later, on Valentine's Day 1993, we stood in front of our fireplace with candles blazing and roses scenting the air. Only five people were in the room—Bill and me, my mom, and a court commissioner friend with power to marry, along with her husband.

Oh, and another was there to witness, the most important one: God.

I didn't yet know Him, but I know now that He was drawing me. Graciously burdening me. Disturbing my internal status quo. Moving me to a spiritual place I'd never been, a place where I considered what *He* might think of my life.

The evening was beautiful, both in the celebration and in my budding consciousness of God. Because of Him, Bill and I had a new status, stepping into words uttered long before—

For this reason a man shall leave his father and his mother, and be joined to his wife; and they shall become one flesh.

Genesis 2:24

Be joined.
Cleave.
Cling.

My relationship with Bill had gone to another level. In the eyes of God, we had a new intimacy, a real intimacy, one that was special and holy. We were *united* in a way we hadn't been earlier. Now that we were joined before God, Bill was my most important relationship. Deep within, I knew we'd taken a divine turn.

But I still didn't quite get it. I'd thought our housing arrangement was the problem. We were "living in sin" and needed to fix it. But sharing a bed didn't make us sinners. Sin was part of my very nature, from birth. Living together was simply one of a thousand outworkings of the sin within.

But though I didn't get it, God did, and He was still working. As I would learn, moving Bill and me to marriage was but a step toward something more glorious. God would soon reveal to me the impact of the cross, that cross that caused me to weep in third grade. I would come to understand what that cross had to do with the Garden of Eden, Adam and Eve, and me. God's love would reach down and make it personal, because that's what He does. He's a God who enjoys relationship, a God who wants us to cling. And by His grace, He leads us to Himself.

Adam and Eve's sin didn't just affect Adam and Eve. When they fell, all of humankind fell. When the first two people were separated from God, it meant every person born after them would be born separated from God.

I find this verse almost chilling:

> *When Adam had lived one hundred and thirty years, he became the father of a son in his own likeness, according to his image, and named him Seth.*

Genesis 5:3

Although Adam's children and the generations born after them would bear the image of God, they would also bear Adam's likeness—the crimson stain of sin.

> *. . . through one man sin entered into the world, and death through sin, and so death spread to all men, because all sinned.*

Romans 5:12

Humanity is not only marked by sin, but by death as well. The two go hand in hand. It's almost hard to fathom, but we are actually born *dead*—spiritually, that is. We come into this world as cute and lovable babies with bodies that will grow, personalities that will take shape, mental capacities that will expand, and innate abilities that will one day shine. But our spirits will not naturally develop on their own. They can't. They're dead.

What does it mean to have a dead spirit? A dead spirit is not alive to God. It does not know God, cannot hear from God, and cannot understand the things of God, including the Word of God. All of which means that a dead spirit cannot cling to God.

But there's more.

In this deadened state, we are not only not alive to God, but very much in tune with the enemy. Our thoughts and desires and our entire mode of living are shaped by him.

And you were dead in your trespasses and sins, in which you formerly walked according to the course of this world, according to the prince of the power of the air, of the spirit that is now working in the sons of disobedience. Among them we too all formerly lived in the lusts of our flesh, indulging the desires of the flesh and of the mind, and were by nature children of wrath, even as the rest.

Ephesians 2:1–3

In this state, we are squarely under the enemy's influence, and there is nothing in us powerful enough to break that hold. From the standpoint of God, we are "children of wrath." Sinners. And there is a penalty for sin: "the wages of sin is death" (Romans 6:23). The only way we can pay the debt of sin we owe is to die, spending an eternity in hell with the enemy, forever separated from God.

I know, this sounds over the top. Bleak. Unnecessarily nightmarish. We are accustomed to language that makes us feel good about ourselves, however we're living our lives. Any notion of judgment and hell is dismissed as folly, or perhaps reserved for the few we deem especially wicked. For the rest, heaven is the automatic destination.

But this is why we need to understand what happened in the beginning of human history. It's also why we need to understand that the enemy is real, that his game is deception, and that his goal is to keep us from relationship with the true and living God. If the devil can squash all talk of judgment and hell, if he can make people think they can live however they want and believe whatever they want and still enjoy an eternity of heavenly bliss—the enemy has won.

But heaven is far from an automatic destination. The truth is this: *none of us* would spend eternity in heaven if left to ourselves. Heaven is not simply the next destination, where we get to hang out and enjoy everything we want to do, on steroids. Heaven is all about *God*, and days are filled with worship and praise and enjoying His presence. Because God is holy, there is no human way anyone, bearing the stain of sin, could show up in heaven and dwell in His presence.

But God made a way, and only one way—the cross. Jesus.

From the beginning, God had a plan to save us. He knew we couldn't save ourselves. He knew sin was hurling us toward permanent death, such that we couldn't be with Him in eternity.

So He sent His Son to die *for us.*

This is amazing! This is love.

"For God so loved the world, that He gave His only begotten Son, that whoever believes in Him shall not perish, but have eternal life."

John 3:16

Some of us know that verse so well that the words have lost their wonder. Please, read them again. Let them reach deep into your soul. Can we even break them down a little?

God so loved the world . . . Though we weren't thinking about God, and the lives we lived weren't pleasing to God, He *loved* us. He didn't cast aside those whom He'd made in His image. He didn't leave us doomed to the clutches of the evil one. Instead, His love moved Him to action.

. . . that He gave His only begotten Son . . . God gave the ultimate. From eternity past, Jesus and the Father are one (John 17:22). *Only* love for us could have moved Him to give His Son, to *watch* His Son—who'd done no wrong—die a brutal death on the cross. God gave that which was precious, sinless, eternal, and inherently mighty, and bid Him die . . . for one reason.

. . . that whoever believes in Him shall not perish . . . God doesn't want us to perish—to remain dead spiritually for all eternity. He created us to live forever with Him, and, though our sin interfered, He still made a way for that to happen. And He didn't give us impossible hoops to jump through—God didn't tell us we could avoid perishing only if we were good enough or worked hard enough. In His amazing grace, He tells us only to repent—turn from our sins—and believe. And in believing, we will not perish . . .

. . . **but have eternal life.** Though our sentence was death, God, in His love and mercy, gives us eternal life when we believe in His Son.

And eternal life is so much more than, "I get to go to heaven someday." Eternal life is *now.* Eternal life is everything changing from the moment you believe, including this—you can now cling to God.

But we hardly understand any of that when we are first saved. I certainly didn't. I had no idea what salvation meant for me, my life, or my relationship with God. But I knew one thing—I wasn't the same.

Almost a year and a half after our Valentine's Day wedding, I found myself visiting a church for the first time—and in tears at the end of the sermon. The visit had unfolded from a whirlwind of events a week before.

I had flown to Los Angeles with a client in the music industry. That was my new thing—entertainment law. I was still practicing litigation at my firm, but I had found something to excite me, not only about the practice of law but about living in Madison, Wisconsin.

To put it mildly, I wasn't fond of Madison. We moved there because Bill had gotten a job offer from the University of Wisconsin. It was the best place for him to start his career as a professor, but I balked from the start. This D.C. girl couldn't get her head around moving to the Cheese State. Besides, my plan was to remain in the Washington area. Forever.

But as God would have it—it's amazing how sovereign He is even when you don't know Him—an economic downturn had closed the door at a D.C. law firm I'd set my heart on joining. Graduation was nearing and I had no job. U.W. offered to shop my resume, and I received an offer from a federal judge who'd been given clearance to hire a third law clerk. It was the best work I could've gotten.

So Bill and I moved, settled in, and loved our jobs—but the lack of diversity in Madison plagued me. I had grown up in a county with the highest percentage of black middle class in the country. Now I was counting black people in the grocery store and the mall, to see if I could get past the fingers on one hand. I complained to Bill every chance I got. Despite our budding careers and the fact that I'd gone on to work for a reputable law firm after the clerkship with the judge, I wanted out. And then Minneapolis happened.

I began handling small entertainment matters for a client in Minneapolis-Saint Paul, a guy who'd been managing my favorite 90s band, Mint Condition. "Popeye" began mentoring me in the music business, and given my passion for R&B music, I was sure this was it. This was why I was in Madison—so I could drive four hours to Minneapolis, network, build an entertainment law specialty, maybe even manage talent myself.

On that weekend in Los Angeles, I'd flown with Popeye to the wedding of "Jimmy Jam" Harris, a Minneapolis-based super-producer. It was the music industry wedding of the year, and my mind was on overload, planning how I would parlay connections I would make with artists and producers into something tangible. When I got home on Sunday, I was excited to tell Bill about the experience—including a one-on-one chat I'd had with Janet Jackson.

Bill was excited too . . . about a church he'd visited that morning.

Over the past couple of years, we'd been attending church in fits and starts. I had a particular motivation: I remembered from Catholic school that God could do miracles, and if He could do miracles, He could get me out of Madison. So I began praying for Him to do so. Then I thought, *If I want God to do something for me, maybe I should do something for Him, like go to church.*

It's amazing how the Lord can use warped motivation and self-centered reasoning to draw us, but He did. In fact, my very dislike of Madison was part of the plan: He used it to turn my thoughts toward Him. However misguided I was, I felt I needed to attend church.

The process was slow going, though. We dipped in and out of Catholic mass, which we'd chosen because it was familiar to us both . . .

and it was short. Even so, we'd skipped church more than we'd gone, and had lately abandoned it altogether.

So I was surprised that Sunday when Bill said he'd visited a new church at the invitation of his barber. He was so enthused he said I just *had* to go the following Sunday. I did, and throughout the entire sermon it was as if my soul stood at attention, soaking in every word, wondering why, at the age of twenty-seven, I'd never heard anything like this. The pastor's passion for God's Word was palpable.

For the second time in my life, I was in tears in a pew . . . because of Jesus.

We didn't miss a Sunday after that. God's love had captured us. Soon I found myself praying a different way—for forgiveness and to give the Lord my life. In the quiet of my home and my heart, I was saved. Born again. But what did that mean exactly?

I honestly couldn't have told you in that moment. But it meant *everything*.

Born again. Many of us heard the words for years before understanding what they mean. In college one of my friends disappeared from the social scene. When I asked about him, the word was that he'd been "born again."

My mind conjured thoughts of church all day Sunday. No parties, no drinking, no secular music. That's what "born again" meant to me. Rules and obligations. I had no clue as to the miracle and the beauty in those words.

We've talked about what happens when we're born into this world. It doesn't matter who our parents are or what the circumstances of our birth are. Our race and socioeconomic status don't factor in, either. We can't escape being born in sin.

But God.

He made a way for us to start over, to be born, "not of blood nor of the will of the flesh nor of the will of man, but of God" (John 1:13). The first time around we were born of natural parents. But "whoever believes that Jesus is the Christ is born of God" (1 John

5:1). We become *His* children (1 John 3:9). And we are indwelt by His Holy Spirit.

It's as if God rewinds back to the beginning, back to "let Us make man in Our image, according to Our likeness" (Genesis 1:26). Just as Adam and Eve were handcrafted, so to speak, believers today are "His workmanship, created in Christ Jesus" (Ephesians 2:10).

That's the miracle and beauty of being born again. We are *re-created* in Christ. We become new creations—"the old things passed away; behold, new things have come" (2 Corinthians 5:17). The sin nature we inherited from Adam still resides within us—we won't be free of that until our earthly bodies are renewed—but we are no longer in the grip of the enemy. We are freed from the power of darkness and sin. We're alive to God. We *belong* to God.

We're in relationship with Him. We can now *cling* to Him. It's amazing that we can have an intimate relationship with God. But it's even more amazing to know that *He* first chose intimacy with us.

3

The God-Side of Intimacy

It was more than fifteen years ago, but I still remember the excitement as we threw our overnight bags into the trunk of the car and started down the highway. My girlfriend and I had six hours of driving ahead of us, but it would pass quickly. We were on our way to a women's conference. *A women's conference.* An entire weekend of awesome worship music, Bible teaching, and fun, late-night fellowship.

We had planned like crazy for this conference. We'd gotten our husbands on board and given them short tutorials on the toddlers—how to get them to eat veggies, how not to mess up their potty training—stocked our refrigerators and bought notebooks and pens. And we'd prayed. More than anything, we wanted God to meet us in a special way.

And He did. The conference was everything we hoped it would be. My friend and I were both on a spiritual high as we worshipped with thousands of women, the music ushering us into sacred space, the teaching hitting our hearts where needed. We laughed. We cried. We chatted and praised.

And we sighed and lamented. The special worship time we'd had, the closeness we'd felt with God . . . was coming to an end. We were headed back to the doldrums of routine, life in the everyday, where we didn't get the highs. Where we didn't feel that kind of closeness.

But we vowed, "Same time next year!" And we began the countdown to the next time we would experience that coveted intimacy with God.

When you think of intimacy with God, you may picture yourself doing the work. God is somewhere distant, waiting. And you must make the effort to move closer to Him, unsure whether He will receive you. Or maybe the idea of intimacy with God is altogether foreign to you. It's for the super-spiritual, for pastors and dedicated missionaries, people who bleed ministry. Or perhaps you equate intimacy, as I did, with an experience that comes only once in a while, programmed and packaged. Church on Sunday may be the time you feel close to God—the other days of the week, not so much.

But it's my prayer that, as believers, we see intimacy with God differently, that it wouldn't be a foreign idea or a once-in-a-while experience for which we must wait. Indeed, that is my heartbeat as I write this book. And rather than regard intimacy as humans doing the work to get close to God, I pray we embrace this beautiful truth—that God has been the One moving *us* toward intimacy with *Him*.

God Chose You Long Ago

I have a fascination with time in the Bible. I like to mark references as to when things are happening ("six days later") or predicted to happen ("when seventy years have been completed"), even if the time reference is purposefully unclear ("of that day and hour no one knows"). But one of my favorite time references is "in the beginning" (Genesis 1:1; John 1:1). And here's one that *really* excites me: *before* the beginning.

God was busy even before He went about the business of creating. He established wisdom *before*.

"The LORD possessed me at the beginning of His way,
Before His works of old.
From everlasting I was established,
From the beginning, from the earliest times of the earth."

Proverbs 8:22–23

Jesus was foreknown and loved by the Father *before.*

For He was foreknown before the foundation of the world, but has appeared in these last times for the sake of you who through Him are believers in God.

1 Peter 1:20–21

"Father, I desire that they also, whom You have given Me, be with Me where I am, so that they may see My glory which You have given Me, for you loved Me before the foundation of the world."

John 17:24

God made promises *before.*

. . . in hope of eternal life, which God, who never lies, promised before the ages began.

Titus 1:2 ESV

And God chose us *before.*

Blessed be the God and Father of our Lord Jesus Christ, who has blessed us with every spiritual blessing in the heavenly places in Christ, just as He chose us in Him before the foundation of the world, that we should be holy and blameless before Him.

Ephesians 1:3–4

Before the foundation of the world. Before God created the heavens and the earth. Before there were sea creatures, creeping things, beasts of the earth, and even people—God chose us in Christ to be in relationship with Him.

That's an incredible truth.

Meditate on it for a moment.

Linger with it:

God chose you for intimacy long ago.

Let's look at another verse that speaks to this fact and deepens our awareness of God's movement toward us. The apostle Peter wrote to believers scattered throughout Asia Minor (the area of modern-day Turkey), and he said this of them:

> . . . who are **chosen** according to the foreknowledge of God the Father, by the sanctifying work of the Spirit . . .
>
> 1 Peter 1:1–2

I find this fascinating. All Scripture is inspired by God (2 Timothy 3:16), which means that when the apostle Paul pointed out early in Ephesians, "He chose us in [Christ]," that was divine inspiration. God wanted us to know that He took personal, direct action concerning us. Likewise, in the opening of Peter's letter, when he used *chosen* as a special identifier for believers, the word was from God. God wanted us to know that that's who we are. We are marked by that identity.

And did you notice what else Peter said? We were "chosen *according to the foreknowledge of God.*" I love that added truth. It moves me to cling all the more, knowing that it was God who first had me in mind.

You might be aware, though, that this topic is much debated. Some say it wasn't that God first chose us. Rather, God looked down through the corridors of time and saw that *we* would choose *Him*—and that's why He chose us. In other words, He had "foreknowledge" of our choice and acted in response.

Don't worry. I have no intention of getting into some lengthy discussion of a topic that could fill a library wing. But here's the thing—the heart of this book is that you and I would choose a lifestyle of intimacy with God. And His choosing us is not so much a lofty theological matter as a deep reflection of His love and grace toward us. It's an irresistible bidding of us to come, which in turn encourages us to respond.

And since, as we'll explore in the next chapter, growth in understanding God's Word is part of clinging, there's no need to shy away from a topic such as this. You and I may not be theologians, but God has given us His Word and the gift of His Spirit to teach us His Word. With prayerful study, He opens up our understanding. So, without getting deep into the weeds, I want to share why I believe the Bible teaches that God chose us of His own accord, purely as a matter of grace. My hope is simply that this will spur us toward praise and a closer walk with Him.

First, God's "choosing" is found throughout His Word, and the emphasis is always on *Him* as the one who chooses.

God chose Abraham.

God Himself says this of Abraham:

> *"For I have **chosen** Him, so that he may command his children and his household after him to keep the way of the LORD by doing righteousness and justice, so that the LORD may bring upon Abraham what He has spoken about him."*

> Genesis 18:19

When God called Abram, he was in Mesopotamia, a land where the people worshipped other gods. Abram didn't know the true God to that point. But when God called him, he obeyed by faith, left his country and his family, and followed the Lord. God changed Abram's name to Abraham and promised that through him all the nations of the earth would be blessed. Abraham was God's sovereign choice for God's purpose.

God chose Jacob over Esau.

When Abraham's son, Isaac, was set to have twins by his wife, Rebekah, "though the twins were not yet born and had not done anything good or bad, so that God's purpose according to His **choice** would stand, not because of works but because of Him who calls, it was said to her, 'The older will serve the younger'" (Romans 9:11–12). Did you notice the language? It de-emphasizes the human element—the twins themselves had done nothing. Instead, the emphasis is on God—*His* purpose, *His* choice, *His* call. The twins were Jacob and Esau. Although Esau was the older brother and typically would have been the favored one, God chose Jacob. It was through Jacob that the people of Israel descended, including, ultimately, God's Son, Jesus.

God chose Israel to be His people.

"For you are a holy people to the LORD your God; the LORD your God has chosen you to be a people for His own possession out of all the peoples who are on the face of the earth. The LORD did not set His love on you nor choose you because you were more in number than any of the peoples, for you were the fewest of all peoples, but because the LORD loved you and kept the oath which He swore to your forefathers, the LORD brought you out by a mighty hand and redeemed you from the house of slavery, from the hand of Pharaoh king of Egypt."

Deuteronomy 7:6–8

As Moses spoke these words to the people of Israel, he made sure they understood that God had chosen them out of all the people in the world—but not because there was anything to recommend them. Rather, God chose them out of love and to keep the promise He'd made to their ancestors Abraham, Isaac, and Jacob, whom He'd also chosen.

God chose the tribe of Levi to minister unto Him.

Of the twelve tribes of Israel, only one—the tribe of Levi—was not given an inheritance in the Promised Land. Instead, the Lord provided for them as the designated priests of the people.

*"For the LORD your God has **chosen** him and his sons from all your tribes, to stand and serve in the name of the LORD forever."*

Deuteronomy 18:5

*"Then the priests, the sons of Levi, shall come near, for the LORD your God has **chosen** them to serve Him and to bless in the name of the LORD."*

Deuteronomy 21:5

It wasn't that the tribe of Levi had distinguished itself as ministers, so as to catch God's notice, nor that they were "holier" than their fellow Israelites. It was purely God's choice.

God chose David to be king.

When God sent the prophet Samuel to anoint the next king of Israel among the sons of Jesse, Samuel was certain God's choice would be the oldest. He took one look at Eliab, and said, "Surely the LORD's anointed is before Him" (1 Samuel 16:6). But God let Samuel know that the oldest wasn't the one. Jesse paraded six more sons before Samuel, to which Samuel replied, "The LORD has not **chosen** these" (1 Samuel 16:10). It was the youngest—the one who was tending sheep and hadn't even been summoned to the gathering—whom God had chosen.

Jesus chose the disciples.

On one occasion during Jesus's ministry on earth, many of His followers left Him. Why? Because they stumbled over statements about who He was and what was required for eternal life. Jesus then turned to the twelve disciples and asked if they would be leaving as well. Peter assured Jesus that they weren't, saying, "We have believed and have come to know that You are the Holy One of God" (John 6:69). Jesus replied:

*"Did I Myself not **choose** you, the twelve, and yet one of you is a devil?"*

John 6:70

What a remarkable demonstration of divine sovereignty. Jesus emphasizes that He *Himself* chose the disciples, including the one who would betray Him: Judas. Jesus knew "from the beginning" that Judas would perform the evil act (John 6:64), but chose him anyway to fulfill divine purpose.

On the night He was arrested, Jesus repeated that He'd chosen the twelve—and also made clear that they had not chosen Him.

> *"You did not **choose** Me but I **chose** you, and appointed you that you would go and bear fruit, and that your fruit would remain, so that whatever you ask of the Father in My name He may give to you. . . . If you were of the world, the world would love its own; but because you are not of the world, but I **chose** you out of the world, because of this the world hates you."*

John 15:16, 19

God's "choosing" is a truth repeated throughout Scripture, a truth that illumines His sovereignty and grace. But let's think about that other view again, of God looking down through the annals of time, seeing that we would choose Him, and thus, choosing us. Who would get the glory in that scenario? *We* would—because we had been so thoughtful and wise as to make the right decision to choose God. Yet the Bible teaches that God will not share His glory with another (Isaiah 42:8).

Moreover, if our salvation hinged on the fact that we were wise enough to choose God—and as a result He chose us—we would be able to boast in our salvation. God intended the very opposite:

> *For by grace you have been saved through faith; and that not of yourselves, it is the gift of God; not as a result of works, so that no one may boast.*

Ephesians 2:8–9

By grace. Through faith. Not of yourselves. Gift of God. Where is God placing emphasis? Does that not move you to praise?

One last point: if we say that God is only reacting to what He knew we would one day do, then we must also be saying that we're *able* to choose Him on our own. But prior to the Spirit's work in salvation, we are *dead* in trespasses and sins, remember? How can we make the holy decision to choose Him when we're dead spiritually? In truth, we weren't thinking about God in that deadened state.

There is none righteous, not even one;
There is none who understands,
There is none who seeks for God;
All have turned aside, together they have become useless;
There is none who does good,
There is not even one.

Romans 3:10–12

The clarity is astounding. None of us can boast about our salvation because none of us were seeking God, none doing anything good. This also means that on our own, none of us could have moved toward intimacy with God. We had all "turned aside."

But God.

Because of His great love for us, He turned us toward Himself and made us alive by grace through faith . . . a plan He purposed long ago. This goodness overwhelms me. He chose intimacy with me and with you—*He* moved toward *us*—and then He gives us grace to move toward Him.

God Sent His Son

With other religions in the world, people must try to make their way toward whomever or whatever is being worshipped. Christianity is unique in that God came to us in human flesh. That God sent His Son to earth was an amazing show of intimacy.

God is spirit, and no man has ever seen Him (John 1:18; 4:24). In the Old Testament, God's presence with His people—His glory—came in the form of a pillar of cloud by day and a pillar of fire by night as the Israelites wandered in the wilderness. During that time, He instructed

Moses to build a portable sanctuary, "that I may dwell among them" (Exodus 25:8). The people consulted the Lord at the tent of meeting, and when Moses entered the tent, "the pillar of cloud would descend and stand at the entrance of the tent; and the LORD would speak with Moses" (Exodus 33:9).

When Moses finished the building project, "the cloud covered the tent of meeting, and the glory of the LORD filled the tabernacle" (Exodus 40:34). Inside the tabernacle was the ark of the covenant, housed in the "holy of holies" beyond a heavy, woven, blue, purple, and scarlet veil. That was where God would appear (Leviticus 16:2)—it could be accessed just once a year, and only by the high priest as he came to offer atonement for sin.

In the days of King Solomon, an elaborate, permanent temple was built. "Then the priests brought the ark of the covenant of the LORD to its place, into the inner sanctuary of the house, to the holy of holies" (2 Chronicles 5:7). When Solomon prayed to dedicate the temple, "the priests could not enter into the house of the LORD because the glory of the LORD filled the LORD's house" (2 Chronicles 7:2). As with the tabernacle, only the high priest could enter this holy of holies—where God's presence was manifested—and only once a year.

But when God's chosen time came, He revealed a greater, more intimate, plan as to how He would dwell among His people. He sent His Son.

And the Word became flesh, and dwelt among us, and we saw His glory, glory as of the only begotten from the Father, full of grace and truth.

John 1:14

Before, God's presence was housed in a tabernacle or temple; now His glory was manifested in human flesh. Before, only one human being had access to His immense glory, once a year; now, multitudes could behold Him and daily receive His care. Jesus, fully God and fully man, chose to dwell with people in a more personal way, to be touched, handled, heard, and seen.

His disciples could break bread with Him (John 13:25). Mary could anoint His feet with perfume and wipe them with her hair (John 12:3). Parents could bring their children so Jesus could lay hands on them and pray for them (Matthew 19:13–15). Even a rich tax collector like Zacchaeus, despised by the people, could experience the intimacy of having Jesus in his home (Luke 19:1–9).

The Gospels are filled with "signs and wonders," the miracles that Jesus performed, testifying that He is the Christ, the Son of God. But also woven throughout the text is His desire for intimacy—a wonder in itself. We see intimacy in His leaving heaven to come to earth. Intimacy in His everyday interactions while ministering on earth. And we see incredible intimacy with His disciples the night before He went to the cross.

Intimacy before the Agony of the Cross

Jesus would be arrested in mere hours and crucified the following day. Awaiting Him was an intense agony, of which He was well aware. Once Jesus had eaten the Passover meal with His disciples, He could have departed to a mountainside alone to pray, as He'd done before. But rather than focus on Himself and the anguish that awaited Him, He focused on relationship.

During supper, Jesus rose to personally wash the feet of His disciples. He stooped before them, one by one, removing the dust and grime. It was so shocking that Peter told Him, "Never shall You wash my feet!" (John 13:8). But Jesus let Peter know that there was symbolism in the cleansing, instructing all the disciples to follow His example. Here was servanthood and humility, and also a tremendous display of intimacy.

Yet, this was only the start of the evening, one unlike any other recorded in the Gospels. After the meal (and after Judas had left to betray Him), Jesus informed the disciples that He was leaving and, for now, they could not follow. Sorrow filled their hearts, but as only their loving Lord could, Jesus reassured them: "I will not leave you as orphans; I will come to you" (John 14:18). In fact, He gave this comfort about the future: "If I go and prepare a place for you, I will come again and receive you to Myself, that where I am, there you may be also" (John 14:3). Meanwhile, He promised that His peace and His love would remain with them, and that they would receive another Helper, the Holy Spirit (John 14:16, 27).

As the hour of His arrest drew near, Jesus lingered with them still, saying, "Get up, let us go from here" (John 14:31). I imagine the disciples' steps were heavy as they processed Jesus's words. He was *leaving* them. They'd been dwelling in close relationship, but now He would be gone. Yes, they would have the Holy Spirit, but they were used to having *Jesus,* in the flesh. What would their days be like when they were separated from Him?

Then He said three words that surely astounded:
Abide in Me (John 15:4).

Though He was leaving, though they could not yet follow, though their relationship would not be the same . . . *they could still be in close relationship.* They could **abide in Him.**

These words weren't for those eleven disciples only; they are for all of us who believe. These are words I love and turn to often. They are akin to those other three words that captured me: "Cling to Him."

But let me finish the sentence, because it only gets more amazing:
Abide in Me, and I in you.

Who would have thought that there could be *more* intimacy with Jesus once He returned to heaven? On earth, He was *with* His followers. Now He is *in* us, wherever we go.

I'm not big on hyperbole, but it actually gets even more amazing.

That same evening, Jesus prayed to the Father for the disciples—as well as for *us*—and the focus of the prayer was oneness.

". . . that they may all be one; even as You, Father, are in Me and I in You, that they also may be in Us."

John 17:21

Why is this even more amazing? In the Old Testament, God says to *cling* to Him. Here in the New Testament, Jesus says to *abide* in Him. In this prayer, Jesus makes clear that He and the Father are One—and we are in *Them*. I'm reminded of "Let us make man in Our image" (Genesis 1:26). God desired from the beginning that we would be like Him. He desired that we would dwell in intimate relationship with Him. Jesus, God in flesh, prayed that we would be one with Him and the Father. And once Jesus ascended to heaven, the Holy Spirit came to indwell believers.

This is the God-side of intimacy. Before we knew God, He knew us. He was already moving toward us, pursuing us. Had already loved us. Had already chosen us. He had a plan for us, a plan for relationship. He sent His Son, and then sent His Spirit. He's made it possible for us to be *in* Him, and He in us. He's given us everything we need to *cling*.

We don't have to wait for a programmed and packaged event. And we certainly don't have to regard the idea of intimacy with God as foreign. By God's grace, we can choose intimacy with Him *daily,* and it begins simply with getting to know Him.

4

Knowing God Intimately

I still remember my first official date with my husband, more than twenty-six years ago. I say "official" because, the week before, Bill and I had connected at a popular restaurant happy hour on the wharf in Washington, D.C. I'd gone with friends to celebrate my twenty-third birthday. He'd shown up with a friend visiting from out of town.

Though I'd known Bill in passing from my college campus, this was the first night we'd actually engaged one another. We danced, talked above the noise in the crowd, and afterward grabbed a meal next door with a mutual friend. At the end of the night, we exchanged numbers and later arranged that "official" date for the following week.

I had little expectation. Relationships had been disappointing lately, and I'd been growing comfortable with the idea of being alone for a season. Really, I was cynical. Bill was nice, fun to be around, and incredibly smart—I'd never met someone pursuing a Ph.D. in mathematics education. But if someone looked good on paper, in my mind I'd better work all the more to uncover what might be wrong. Our date wasn't so much about having a good time as it was a fact-finding investigation.

Over a seafood platter, the exploration began. Who *was* this guy? What was his family background? How did he get from Chicago, where he'd been raised, to grad school in Maryland? What were his plans and goals? His interests? And did he really love math? How did *that* happen?

The more I came to know, the more I wanted to know. Extended phone calls followed that date. And more dinners. And more questions. I was moving from a surface knowledge of Bill to deeper layers, and every layer inspired more exploration. In natural fashion, time with him led to knowledge of him. And knowledge of him led to close relationship.

It couldn't have happened any other way. Any intimate friendship takes time, time in which we cultivate a knowledge of one another. Imagine having a best friend about whom you know little. You don't know her story—where she's been, things she's done. You don't know her heart—what she adores, what she can do without. You don't know that beneath her cavalier exterior is a sensitive spirit that cries over the sappiest movies.

I'm sure you're thinking what I'm thinking—*then she's not your best friend.* The two of you are not close. There's no intimacy.

Intimacy with God is no different. We can be in relationship with God through His Son, saved and secure in our eternal future yet not dwelling closely with Him here on earth. We can know Him in a salvation sense, but not truly *know* Him.

But the richness comes with the *knowing.* Day-to-day peace and joy come with knowing. Staying anchored and abounding and rejoicing in the midst of trials and tribulations come with knowing. And intimacy with God absolutely comes with knowing.

How does all this "knowing" take place? Through the Word of God. Clinging to God doesn't happen apart from clinging to His Word. That's how we grow to know Him deeply. As we saw in the last chapter, He *wants* us to dwell closely with Him. He's put everything in place for us to dwell closely with Him. And that included giving us His Word.

God reveals much about Himself in the Bible. In sixty-six books, we have a treasure trove of knowledge about God—His sovereignty and might, His likes and dislikes, His plans and purposes, His thoughts and even His emotions. In choosing a lifestyle of intimacy, we are choosing to open the Book and discover what God has made known about Himself—indeed, what He *wants* us to know.

I shared a little about how I developed a close relationship with Bill. I'd love also to share something about my journey of growing closer to the Lord.

When I was saved, I knew next to nothing about God. I knew that Jesus died for me on the cross and rose again. I knew John 3:16, I think. And I knew a smattering of Bible stories from Catholic school. Well, I can't actually claim to have known the stories. Just a few facts—Jesus walked on water, turned water to wine, healed the sick, and raised the dead. Apart from being instructed to do so in a class or church setting, I had never actually picked up a Bible to read it—and I was twenty-seven.

After joining my first church in Madison, Wisconsin, the Bible slowly became part of my world. In addition to Sunday worship, where the pastor was going through the book of John, I started going to Sunday school, where he was moving sequentially through Mark. I enjoyed the opportunity to ask questions and build my understanding in the class setting.

But the more I learned, the more I knew how much I didn't know. I'd been introduced to John and Mark, but the balance of the Bible remained a mystery to me. I wasn't reading at home and wasn't really confident in my ability to understand if I did. But a desire grew for additional instruction.

Early on, I'd read an announcement in the church program: "Christian Women Supporting Women meets on Wednesday evenings at 5:00 p.m." I glossed over it for months, until I learned that the focus was Bible study. And since it was led by Marilyn Parks, a woman who had become a "Madison mom" to Bill and me, I decided to give it a try.

In early 1995, I walked through the church doors at midweek for the first time, into the church lounge where Marilyn and one other woman were reading the Bible. No one had ever attended Christian Women on a regular basis. Most weeks Marilyn had sat alone, ready to instruct, waiting for warm bodies.

I joined in the study. Marilyn took her time reading a selected passage, explaining the seventeenth-century King James language, letting us know how it applied to our lives. I was in full pupil mode, soaking in every considered word that passed her lips.

Work obligations caused me to miss meetings here and there, but Christian Women soon became a highlight of my week. I attended for close to five years, even co-leading the sessions after Marilyn moved away. I was reading the Bible in the group and in preparation for the group, but for the most part, my understanding was only in bits and pieces. Still, I was growing closer to God. I wouldn't have called it *intimate*. I'm not sure I knew it *could* be intimate. But that would change.

The turning point came when we moved to Dallas, Texas, in 2000. At North Dallas Community Bible Fellowship, our new church home, I encountered the Bible as never before. The senior pastor and assistant pastors not only taught Scripture in a careful and systematic manner, they made sure that church members had a fundamental understanding of the faith. They required us to attend a new member's orientation, and it was there that I realized how little I understood the truths that undergirded my faith and the Bible as a whole. Afterward, I bombarded the assistant pastors with questions, and they were patient and gracious to put up with me for three hours.

I couldn't sleep that night. Some of the biblical truth they imparted I'd never heard before; some of it contradicted what I'd heard. A hunger came over me that wouldn't let me rest. I wanted to know truth for myself. I wanted a deeper understanding of the Bible. *I wanted a deeper understanding of my God.*

The very next day I found a book on the shelf that I didn't know we had: *How to Study Your Bible* by Kay Arthur. I read it that same day and headed to the store to buy an inductive study Bible, which the book recommended. During my toddlers' naptimes, I sat at my kitchen table with a cup of coffee and started in the first chapter of Genesis. The moment was so pivotal that I dated it in my Bible—July 2000.

I studied every day, line upon line, chapter upon chapter, book upon book. Taking my time, I'd spend days on one chapter, marking key words, jotting in the margin. I became enamored with maps of ancient places, needing to know how far Abram's Ur was from Canaan, Jesus's Judea from Galilee. I drew family trees, noted action verbs, made lists of comparisons and contrasts. I never knew I could fall so deeply in love with the Word, but it was happening. Often I would pause and shake my head at the wonder of a single verse and all that it was teaching me.

Falling in love with the Word led inevitably to drawing closer to the Lord. After all, He's the main character, the presence on every page, the one who breathed it into being and keeps every word alive. As God spoke to Joshua and young Samuel, answered Hannah's prayer and renewed Naomi's hope, joined three Hebrew boys in the fire and shut the mouths of lions, I was with Him, learning of Him.

When God put on flesh and walked the earth, I was with Martha's sister, Mary, as she listened at His feet; in the crowd as bread and fish multiplied; and with His mother, Mary, watching Him hang on the cross. With the turn of every page, my walk with Him deepened, as did my love.

That journey of serious study began more than sixteen years ago and continues even now. Time in the Word of God is still the most cherished part of my day. He is faithful to meet me there. And no matter how many times I've read the same passage, He opens up my understanding to reveal more about Himself. We will never know Him fully this side of heaven, and that's actually good news. It means we get to go deeper and deeper, drawing closer and closer, and the journey will never grow old.

I could not cling to God apart from the knowledge of Him through His Word. Clinging helps us to live above our circumstances. Life brings unexpected twists and turns, but in the midst of them, we can cling to what we know for sure about God. Whatever circumstances may arise, I find myself calling to mind what I know about God—His ways, His heart, and His sovereignty.

Knowing His Ways

In February 2014 I visited Israel for the first time, and I had the opportunity to bring back an engraved piece of jewelry as a souvenir. I ordered a ring with these words inscribed in Hebrew:

Show me Your ways, O Lord; Teach me Your paths.

It's a prayer of David from Psalm 25, one I've prayed for years. Through the prophet Isaiah, God tells us that His ways are higher than our ways, and His thoughts than our thoughts (Isaiah 55:8–9). He could have left it at that, just giving us the bare knowledge that we could never hope to understand Him. He's too far above. One day in heaven maybe we'll learn more.

But He didn't do that. It strikes me deeply that God would be willing to *show* us His ways and *teach* us His paths, through His Word. Indeed, He expects His people to learn His ways. This was God's indictment of the Israelites who wandered in the wilderness for forty years:

"For forty years I loathed that generation,
And said they are a people who err in their heart,
And they do not know My ways."

Psalm 95:10

Thus, when the new generation was set to enter the Promised Land, God's word to them was this:

*"Now, Israel, what does the LORD your God require from you, but to fear the LORD your God, **to walk in all His ways** and love Him, and to serve*

> the LORD *your God with all your heart and with all your soul, and to keep* the LORD's *commandments and His statutes which I am commanding you today for your good?"*

Deuteronomy 10:12–13

Hundreds of years later, David must have been aware of this command. And he knew that in order to walk in God's ways, he had to know them. So this man after God's heart prayed, "Show me Your ways." How interesting, then, that we learn much of God's ways from the life of David.

God's Ways in the Story of David and Goliath

David had been anointed the next king of Israel, but for the moment, Saul still ruled. So David went back to doing what he'd been doing—tending sheep. But while the young shepherd worked, Israel's army was being threatened by a mighty enemy. The Philistines had come against them for battle, led by their champion Goliath, a fearsome giant over nine feet tall, with bronze armor head to toe, a bronze javelin, and a fifteen-pound spear to boot. Goliath challenged the Israelites to choose one man to fight. If that man could kill Goliath, the Philistines would become Israel's servants. But if Goliath prevailed, the Israelites would serve the Philistines. Israel's army was struck with fear (1 Samuel 17:1–11).

David happened upon this tense scene. His father had sent him to take food to his three oldest brothers, who served in Israel's army, and he arrived just in time to see Goliath taunting once again with his challenge. David saw his countrymen's fear as they ran from the giant.

He was incensed. "Who is this uncircumcised Philistine, that he should taunt the armies of the living God?" (1 Samuel 17:26).

David asked what would be done for the man who killed Goliath. Eliab, his oldest brother, gave an angry retort:

"Why have you come down? And with whom have you left those few sheep in the wilderness? I know your insolence and the wickedness of your heart; for you have come down in order to see the battle."

1 Samuel 17:28

We can understand Eliab's anger, I suppose. He had been terrified of this giant, having to flee from his wrath—and here was his baby brother, a mere sheepherder, daring to inquire into the business of warriors. Eliab thought his sneer would discourage David. But David kept asking around and soon found himself in the presence of King Saul, declaring that *he* would fight Goliath.

Saul, like Eliab, thought David must be crazy. The king told him, "You are not able to go against this Philistine to fight with him; for you are but a youth while he has been a warrior from his youth" (1 Samuel 17:33).

But Saul couldn't discourage him either. David replied:

"Your servant was tending his father's sheep. When a lion or a bear came and took a lamb from the flock, I went out after him and attacked him, and rescued it from his mouth; and when he rose up against me, I seized him by his beard and struck him and killed him."

1 Samuel 17:34–35

David stated his résumé matter-of-factly, but you can't help but pause, and say, *Really, David?* Who goes after a lion or a bear, two of the most vicious animals on the planet? People run from them, or try to crouch down and hide. But not David. To rescue his sheep, he *attacked* the lion and bear, and when the animals turned against him, David killed them.

But David knew he wasn't operating in his own strength. "The LORD who delivered me from the paw of the lion and from the paw of the bear, He will deliver me from the hand of this Philistine" (1 Samuel 17:37).

Why couldn't Eliab or Saul discourage David?

Because David knew his God.

David had been clinging to God.

While he was tending his "few sheep in the wilderness," David had been cultivating a close relationship with God. He'd learned much about God's ways.

David knew that God is trustworthy. He *had* to trust God even to think about going after a lion or bear.

David knew that God is faithful. God, who was David's Shepherd (Psalm 23), was with David as he shepherded his sheep.

David knew that God is a deliverer.

Knowing God helped David cling to God, and in doing so, he was built up in courage and strength. With Saul's go-ahead, David proceeded to his one-on-one battle with Goliath, stopping first at a brook to pick up five smooth stones for his sling. He carried a stick as well. That and David's youth infuriated Goliath, who couldn't wait to tear this boy apart. "Come to me, and I will give your flesh to the birds of the sky and the beasts of the field," Goliath said (1 Samuel 17:44).

David didn't flinch. Goliath had a sword, a spear, and a javelin, but that was nothing compared to the living God. God would deliver the giant into the shepherd boy's hands, David said, so that "all the earth may know that there is a God in Israel" (1 Samuel 17:46). What's more, everyone there needed to recognize that God "does not deliver by sword or spear; for the battle is the LORD's" (17:47).

David knew that God desired glory in the earth.

David knew that God does not deliver by human strength or manmade weapons.

David knew that God fights for His people.

Knowing the ways of His God, David ran quickly to the battle line, took a stone and slung it. The stone sank into Goliath's forehead, causing him to fall face-forward to the ground, and David finished him off with the sword. With Goliath dead, the Philistines fled.

From his days as a shepherd boy and in fighting Goliath, David learned much about God's ways. We can also learn much from reading these accounts in God's Word. We see God's faithfulness on the pages, and knowing God in this way moves us to cling to Him—such that we too gain strength and courage to face our daily battles.

God's Ways When David Was on the Run

King Saul's rejoicing over the Philistine victory was short-lived. When he heard the people praising David more than they praised him, Saul became angry. It wasn't long before Saul had declared David his enemy.

Twice Saul hurled a spear at David to pin him to the wall (1 Samuel 18:11). The king then sent messengers to David's house to put him to death, but he escaped through a window (1 Samuel 19:11–12). David had to flee, and he stayed on the run from Saul for years, hiding in caves and strongholds in the wilderness. Saul was relentless, often pursuing David himself, along with three thousand men.

But twice David had an opportunity to kill Saul. At one point David was hiding in the very cave that Saul entered for the purpose of relieving himself. David's men encouraged him to kill Saul; instead, David secretly cut off the edge of Saul's robe. Yet even that bothered David's conscience. After Saul left the cave, David called out to get his attention. Bowing to the ground, David told the king that he could have killed him but didn't, because Saul was the Lord's anointed. "May the Lord judge between you and me, and may the Lord avenge me on you; but my hand shall not be against you" (1 Samuel 24:12).

On another occasion Saul had gone looking for David, but David found him first, sleeping with his spear stuck in the ground near his head. Again David's men encouraged him to kill Saul. But he said, "As the Lord lives, surely the Lord will strike him, or his day will come that he dies, or he will go down into battle and perish. The Lord forbid that I should stretch out my hand against the Lord's anointed" (1 Samuel 26:10–11).

What did David know about God to take such an unusual stance? **David knew that God is the one who avenges.**

David knew that God is sovereign.

David knew that the Lord repays each man according to his righteousness.

Still, this was a very difficult period. David had been given a promise that he would be Israel's next king, but years had passed—and the threat of death was ever at hand. Yet it was during this time that David learned much of God's ways. David had to cling to Him as never before. The psalms he wrote during this period bear witness.

In Psalm 63, while David was hiding in the wilderness, he said his soul thirsted for God, and he sought God earnestly. Despite his plight, he was determined to give praise because "Your lovingkindness is better than life" (Psalm 63:3). What a beautiful testimony of God's ways, that He not only extends lovingkindness but so lavishly that it's better than life itself. David may have been on the run, but God was right with him, making His presence known. David also said:

> *When I remember You on my bed,*
> *I meditate on You in the night watches,*
> *For you have been my help,*
> *And in the shadow of Your wings I sing for joy.*
> *My soul **clings** to You;*
> *Your right hand upholds me.*
>
> Psalm 63:6–8

One normally cannot sing for joy while under severe trial. But David was *clinging*, just as he'd done as a shepherd boy. Did you notice how he maintained a posture of clinging? He was *meditating* on God, remembering. God had been his help with the lion and the bear, with Goliath and the Philistines, and now God was helping with David's own king, Saul. In calling to mind God's ways in the past, David could cling with an abiding trust, knowing that God's right hand, His hand of power, was upholding him.

David gives us more nuggets of God's ways, all written during his time on the run from Saul:

- "Behold, God is my helper; the LORD is the sustainer of my soul" (Psalm 54:4).
- "This I know, that God is for me" (Psalm 56:9).
- "I will cry to God Most High, to God who accomplishes all things for me. He will send from heaven and save me; He reproaches him who tramples upon me. God will send forth His lovingkindness and His truth" (Psalm 57:2–3).
- "I sought the LORD, and He answered me, and delivered me from all my fears" (Psalm 34:4).
- "They who seek the LORD shall not be in want of any good thing" (Psalm 34:10).
- "The eyes of the LORD are toward the righteous and His ears open to their cry" (34:15).
- "The LORD is near to the brokenhearted and saves those who are crushed in spirit" (34:18).

After David ran, hid, and cried out to God for years, the threat of Saul was no more. Killed in another battle against the Philistines, Saul's end was as David had predicted—by the sovereign hand of God. David became the next king of Israel.

David learned that we must wait for God, and that God keeps His promises.

There are such great lessons for us from this period of David's life. We all endure trials and tribulations at one point or another. We have times when we feel dry and weary, when we thirst for God. We endure seasons of brokenheartedness, maybe even betrayal. An intimate knowledge of God's ways makes all the difference.

We want to know that He's there, whether we "feel" Him or not. We want to know that He's able to sustain us, to provide the shelter of His wings in the midst. We want to know that we can rest and not despair. We want to know that He is *for* us. We want to know that even as we wait, He is accomplishing all things for us, and that He's a God who keeps His promises. This is the kind of knowing that strengthens our ability to cling.

Knowing His Heart, in Jeremiah

From the first time I studied the book of Jeremiah, those fifty-two chapters grabbed me. The book has become a favorite of mine. I was drawn to the prophet, to the way he'd steadfastly cling to God. He'd been given such a difficult task: God had called him to tell the people of Israel that judgment was not only coming, it was imminent. They needed to lay aside their idol worship and return to God with their whole hearts. But the people wouldn't listen. At one point, they beat Jeremiah and put him in the stocks. His own trusted friends turned against him.

Jeremiah voiced his hurt and frustration to God. "I have become a laughingstock all day long," he said. "Everyone mocks me" (Jeremiah 20:7). It got so bad that he cursed the day he was born (20:14). Yet Jeremiah also said this:

> *But if I say, "I will not remember Him*
> *Or speak anymore in His name,"*
> *Then in my heart it becomes like a burning fire*
> *Shut up in my bones;*
> *And I am weary of holding it in,*
> *And I cannot endure it.*

Jeremiah 20:9

Jeremiah could have refused to follow God. Like the prevailing attitude of his people, he could have chosen his own way. Instead, he chose God's way. Despite the hardship and rejection, he chose to cling.

But as much as I love the prophet himself in the book of Jeremiah, I especially love what we learn about the heart of God. Hundreds of years before, God had delivered the people of Israel from slavery in Egypt. He had shown them great signs and wonders. In the wilderness, they had pledged themselves to one another. God had said:

> *"You yourselves have seen what I did to the Egyptians, and how I bore you*
> *on eagles' wings, and brought you to Myself. Now then, if you will indeed*

obey My voice and keep My covenant, then you shall be My own possession
among all the peoples, for all the earth is Mine."

Exodus 19:4–5

In response,

All the people answered together and said, "All that the Lord has spoken
we will do!"

Exodus 19:8

That vow (and others that were spoken) meant something to God. He says in Jeremiah, "I remember concerning you the devotion of your youth, the love of your betrothals . . ." (Jeremiah 2:2).

Did you notice the heart of God for relationship? The intimate language? *Devotion. Love. Betrothals.*

But then,

Thus says the Lord,
"What injustice did your fathers find in Me,
That they went far from Me
And walked after emptiness and became empty?"

Jeremiah 2:5

Instead of remaining devoted—instead of clinging to God—Israel strayed in her disobedience. And God wants to know why. *What did I do? Why did you leave Me?*

Clearly, God knew the blame did not lie with Him. He'd done everything for the people of Israel. God was asking the question so that the people would search their own hearts. In doing so, He revealed *His* heart. And amazingly, given that He is the God of the universe, it's a heart that is broken.

In speaking of their "betrothal" and of analogies to husband and wife (Jeremiah 3:1), God painted an image of Himself as the spurned husband and Israel as the unfaithful wife. He had loved and cared for her, protected her, and blessed her. He had been faithful. And yet, "Surely as a woman treacherously departs from her lover, so you have dealt treacherously with Me" (Jeremiah 3:20).

We immediately know how this feels. Even if we've never experienced it personally, we can imagine the pain of a spouse's betrayal. We know what this would do to our heart. God gives us this imagery so that we can understand how He feels.

Still, despite Israel's unfaithfulness, God said, "I thought, 'After she has done all these things she will return to Me'; but she did not return" (Jeremiah 3:7).

Imagine God waiting. The long-suffering. He sees all, so nothing was hidden. Every bit of betrayal unfolded before His eyes. Day after day. For years and years. Yet His arms remained wide open to receive them again.

Even at this point, He pleaded through Jeremiah:

"Return, faithless Israel," declares the Lord;
"I will not look upon you in anger.
For I am gracious," declares the Lord.

Jeremiah 3:12

Again and again He said: "Return" (Jeremiah 3:14; 4:1). He even added, "Return . . . I will heal your faithlessness" (Jeremiah 3:22).

Does your heart not ache along with God's? He offers grace and healing in the midst of His own disappointment. This too is the heart of God, for us all.

But the people did not return to Him. Judgment for sin had to come, for "those whom the Lord loves He disciplines" (Hebrews 12:6). The land God had given His people was now given into the hands of King Nebuchadnezzar and his Babylonian army. Babylon captured Jerusalem, laid siege to the city, broke down the walls, burned the temple of God and every house in Jerusalem, executed priests and leaders, and carried thousands into exile (Jeremiah 52).

Jeremiah, favored by God, was allowed to remain in Jerusalem with others left behind. But this also meant he was confronted daily with devastation, affliction, and homelessness. The book of Lamentations records Jeremiah's grief over the fall of Jerusalem. He knew God had allowed the desolation, and in vivid language Jeremiah described his plight, saying at one point, "He has caused my flesh and my skin to waste away, He has broken my bones. He has besieged and encompassed me with bitterness and hardship" (Lamentations 3:4–5).

But at his lowest point, devoid of strength and peace, Jeremiah's soul remembered what he knew about God—and he found hope. This is what he called to mind:

> *The LORD's lovingkindnesses indeed never cease,*
> *For His compassions never fail.*
> *They are new every morning;*
> *Great is Your faithfulness.*

Lamentations 3:22–23

Jeremiah knew God's heart—full of lovingkindness and compassion. Every morning, new mercies. Ever and always—faithfulness. These truths brought Jeremiah comfort in the midst of grief. Jeremiah knew that in God's faithfulness, He had to judge sin. Yet also in His faithfulness, the people were not forsaken. God's plans and purposes toward them would yet be established. Knowing God's heart kept Jeremiah clinging when everything around him had fallen apart.

The same applies to us today. Circumstances are ever changing. We are troubled, thrown into confusion by happenings in our world and nation, among friends and family, and in our lives personally. There is always much we don't know or understand, and one of the biggest questions we often have is why God allowed a particular thing to happen.

But, like Jeremiah, we need to call to mind what we *do* know about the heart of God, so that from the depths of our own hearts, we can cling.

Knowing His Heart, through Jesus

I love the Gospels. I love walking with Jesus as He walked here on earth. I love seeing how He interacted with leaders and beggars, Jews and

Gentiles, those grieved by sin and those steeped in self-righteousness. I follow Him through the Gospels and worship, pause, ponder, pray, stand amazed, smile, and laugh—not a *ha ha* laugh, but that awed laugh that says, "Your ways and Your wisdom are *so* far above." All the while, I am learning His heart.

Many prefer the kind, servant heart of Jesus to the God of the Old Testament who judges sin—as if they are polar opposites. But Jesus and the Father are one, and thus, the heart of one reflects the heart of the other. We see the patient, gracious heart of the Father in the Old Testament (as in the book of Jeremiah), and in the New Testament we read that Jesus will return to judge humankind.

Still, only in the Gospels do we see God in flesh. By walking with Jesus through the Gospels, we come to know Him in an intimate way—like the apostle Paul counting all things loss "in view of the surpassing value of knowing Christ Jesus my Lord" (Philippians 3:8)—and we find ourselves clinging to Him, especially in life's crucial moments.

I remember vividly such a moment, shortly after we moved to Saint Louis and began homeschooling. Interestingly, I had prayed that God would never call me to homeschool. I'd met a homeschool mom of six in Dallas, and as she described her day, my head began to swim. *Never could I take that on,* I thought, *even with two.*

I'd left my law firm three years before to be home with my little ones—but also to write. And I'd been looking forward to the day when both kids were in school and the writing process would be easier. My first book had been published, and I was ready to get going with the next. But I'd quickly learned that being a full-time mom of toddlers and full-time writer were not compatible.

We were moving to Saint Louis, though, and things would be different. The kids were registered for first grade and preschool. My own pencils were sharpened to get back into the writing game. Until late that summer, that is, when the Lord moved in my heart to homeschool.

Everywhere I turned, homeschooling was before me. And I began praying for my educator husband to see the benefits. The Lord answered. By fall, both kids were learning at home and thriving. I'd embraced it with gusto. I knew without a doubt that the path was God-ordained.

But I had a moment.

It hit me one day that life was nowhere near what I'd envisioned. I thought God had called me to write, but it had been years since I'd had time. And now that I was homeschooling, books might never happen. Was this all there was? Would I never do the things that had long been on my heart to do? How long would I have to sacrifice?

As emotion rose and self-pity crept in, a verse began to swirl in my mind. I couldn't recall the words exactly, but Jesus had said something about a grain of wheat. I got my Bible and found it:

"Truly, truly, I say to you, unless a grain of wheat falls into the earth and dies, it remains alone; but if it dies, it bears much fruit."

John 12:24

I read that verse again and again. The words were a lifeline, beckoning me to grab hold. I was reminded of Jesus, King Eternal, Lord of all, who had laid down His life for *me*. That was true sacrifice. True love.

These verses came to mind as well:

Do not merely look out for your own personal interests but also for the interests of others. Have this attitude in yourselves which was also in Christ Jesus, who, although He existed in the form of God, did not regard equality with God a thing to be grasped, but emptied Himself, taking the form of a bond-servant, and being made in the likeness of men. Being found in appearance as a man, He humbled Himself by becoming obedient to the point of death, even death on a cross.

Philippians 2:4–8

A heart of servitude. A heart of humility. A heart of obedience. And Jesus was calling me to imitate His example. If He could set aside His rights as *God* and sacrifice His very life for *me*, how could I not give up a dream of my heart for the sake of my family?

Tears fell from my eyes. *Lord, I don't care if I never write another book. Help me to die to self and to anything that is not Your will. I pray to bear much fruit, right here in my home.*

We have no greater example to follow than Jesus. Clinging to Him and all that He is gives us a higher perspective, an eternal perspective. It doesn't change our circumstance, it changes *us.*

And that clinging is fueled by knowing Him. What an immense blessing that He put on human flesh and came to earth to be *known.* Knowing Jesus is a privilege to embrace continually.

Grow in the grace and knowledge of our Lord and Savior Jesus Christ.

2 Peter 3:18

Knowing His Sovereignty

If there is one attribute of God that causes me to cling to Him *no matter what*, it is that He is sovereign. Where His sovereignty is on grand display in my Bible, I've drawn boxes around passages and put notes in the margin so I can find them quickly when I need them—and cling.

One of my favorite "sovereign" passages relates to Ahab, who was ruler of the northern kingdom of Israel. (After King Solomon died, Israel divided into two rival nations, a northern kingdom that kept the name Israel and a southern kingdom called Judah.) Ahab was wicked, more wicked than any of the kings who'd come before him. Added to that, he married Jezebel, daughter of a Sidonian king, and worshipped Jezebel's false god, Baal.

Because of the king's wickedness, he became well acquainted with the prophet Elijah, who was sent by God more than once to pronounce judgment upon Ahab. It was during Ahab's reign that Elijah challenged the prophets of Baal to a test: they would call on the name of their god, and Elijah would call on the name of his God, and whoever answered by fire would be the true God. The prophets of Baal called out from morning till evening and got no response.

Elijah called on the name of the Lord, and fire fell from heaven, consuming the offering he'd placed on the altar—and drenched with water (1 Kings 18:20–40)! Elijah then slew the four hundred fifty prophets of Baal, earning for himself a death sentence from Jezebel (1 Kings 19:1–2).

Sometime later, King Ahab decided to go to war against Aram. He enlisted the help of Jehoshaphat, leader of the southern kingdom of Judah. Jehoshaphat first wanted to inquire of God (1 Kings 22:5). Was it God's will for the two kings to go to war?

Ahab assembled four hundred prophets, all of whom said, "Go up, for the Lord will give it into the hand of the king" (1 Kings 22:6).

Jehoshaphat didn't find the four hundred convincing. He said, "Is there not yet a prophet of the LORD here, that we may inquire of him?" (1 Kings 22:7).

Ahab's response is somewhat amusing: "There is yet one man by whom we may inquire of the LORD, but I hate him, because he does not prophecy good concerning me, but evil" (1 Kings 22:8).

Ah, so Ahab *did* know of a true prophet—yet he paraded four hundred men who would tickle his ears. Ahab thought he could avoid the sovereign will of God, simply by not hearing it spoken. Reluctantly, he called forth the true prophet, Micaiah.

The scene was impressive, with King Ahab and King Jehoshaphat seated on thrones at the city gate, majestic in royal robes, with hundreds of prophets assuring them that God would give victory. Enter Micaiah. He was urged by the man who'd escorted him, "Please let your word be like the word of one of [Ahab's prophets], and speak favorably" (1 Kings 22:13).

But Micaiah had another objective—to cling to God. Despite overwhelming pressure to conform, he knew that these kings were sovereign only in a limited way, over limited territory. Micaiah's allegiance was to the One who was sovereign over all. So he replied, "As the LORD lives, what the LORD says to me, that I shall speak" (1 Kings 22:14).

Micaiah told King Ahab that he saw all Israel scattered, like sheep with no shepherd (1 Kings 22:17). Ahab knew what this meant. It prophesied his doom.

But Micaiah wasn't done. He gave a rare behind-the-scenes glimpse into God's sovereignty unfolding in heaven:

> *"Therefore, hear the word of the LORD. I saw the LORD sitting on His throne, and all the host of heaven standing by Him on His right and on His left. The LORD said, 'Who will entice Ahab to go up and fall at Ramoth-gilead?' And one said this while another said that. Then a spirit came forward and stood before the LORD and said, 'I will entice him.' The LORD said to him, 'How?' And he said, 'I will go out and be a deceiving spirit in the mouth of all his prophets.' Then He said, 'You are to entice him and also prevail. Go and do so.' Now therefore, behold, the LORD has put a deceiving spirit in the mouth of all these your prophets; and the LORD has proclaimed disaster against you."*

1 Kings 22:19–23

How astounding! While Ahab and Jehoshaphat were seated on their thrones, the God of heaven and earth was on *His* throne, directing all that transpired before them. God was sovereign over the words of Micaiah *and* over the words that came from the false prophets' mouths. As Jesus demonstrated time and again during His earthly ministry, demons are subject to God. Here, God allowed demon spirits to speak through false prophets to induce Ahab to go to war, where he would die.

King Ahab ordered Micaiah to be thrown in prison until he returned safely from battle. Having heard God's sovereign plan, Ahab came up with his own plan to circumvent it. He told Jehoshaphat to wear his kingly robes into battle, but Ahab would disguise himself.

Ahab's instincts were spot-on. The king of Aram had told his men not to fight with anyone but the king of Israel. But since Ahab was disguised, they didn't know who he was. At one point, the Arameans steered their chariots toward Jehoshaphat, thinking he was Ahab. But once again, God is sovereign: Jehoshaphat's death was not appointed for that day. When Jehoshaphat cried out, "the LORD helped him, and God diverted them from him" (2 Chronicles 18:31).

Ahab surely thought he'd outmaneuvered not only the Aramean army but God Himself. He was in the battle, fighting in his chariot, dressed in protective—and disguising—armor. No one could find him to target him.

Except God.

This sentence is marked in my Bible:

Now a certain man drew his bow at random and struck the king of Israel in a joint of the armor.

1 Kings 22:34

Is that not amazing? With God there is no such thing as "at random." God is sovereign over "coincidence," "chance," and "at random." It was random to the man who drew his bow. But God guided that arrow straight to the joint—*a narrow little crack!*—where it could penetrate in a lethal way. Ahab died that evening, as God had said.

I turn to this passage often. When winds begin to kick up in my life and threaten to push me off course, I need to be reminded that God is sovereign over *everything*. He is on His throne, watching, directing, working. He is in control always.

Knowing God is sovereign moves me to cling to Him. I can *trust* Him. Whatever has blown into my life may have taken me by surprise, but God is never taken by surprise. He allowed the winds for a purpose, and if He can direct a random arrow into a joint of a king's armor, He can surely establish His purpose in my life. Clinging to Him keeps me from being tossed in such times.

But clinging is not just for the storms of life. As we rear our children, as we engage in evangelism and ministry, as we pray for needed direction, as we endure seasons of waiting . . . knowing that God is sovereign is an ever-present comfort, peace, assurance, hope, and joy. Knowing God is sovereign keeps us clinging to Him, the only one who knows the end from the beginning.

5

Making Prayer a Lifestyle

I am not a prayer warrior. I reserve that designation for people like my mom. It is nothing for her to wake up at three in the morning and intercede for hours for those whom the Lord puts on her heart. She's retired and lives alone, and the Lord uses her to minister to many through prayer.

I'm not a prayer journaler either—at least not a faithful one. I love the idea, and I have loads of pretty (albeit empty) journals I couldn't resist. Each was bought with grand plans that *this time* I would stick to it and be blessed by a faithful recording of prayer requests and their answers. But if you checked my current journal, you'd see a burst of activity over several days, maybe weeks—then nothing for months, followed by another burst of activity . . .

My "war room" seems to be following suit. The 2015 movie by that name spurred me to transform a basement bathroom into a dedicated prayer space. I got an area rug to throw on the dank floor and found a basket-weaved set of drawers on clearance for (ahem) prayer journals, a Bible, notebooks, and pens. I put a spare chair in the corner and verses of Scripture, hand carved on wood, on the walls. Inspired, I went down faithfully for weeks—until it got cold. Determined still, I trekked down with a space heater, which helped for a little while . . . until I saw a giant spider who'd found shelter from the cold in my war room. I haven't been down since. It's been over a month.

You probably guessed that this chapter is not a how-to on prayer. Countless books have been written on the subject and, clearly, I am no expert. But that's the thing: it's not about being an expert. It's not about praying a certain way or saying the right things in the right place with the right posture. I simply hope to encourage you toward a lifestyle of prayer, which goes hand in hand with choosing a lifestyle of intimacy with God.

For each of us as believers, our prayer lives will look different. But one thing is commanded of us all—"pray without ceasing" (1 Thessalonians 5:17). That may seem a burdensome expectation, maybe even an impossible one. But it's encouraging that this is God's call because it means He wants us to come to Him. To dwell with Him. Share with Him. Depend on Him. Love Him enough to *talk* to Him.

Naturally, "pray without ceasing" does not imply uninterrupted twenty-four-hour prayer. It signifies regularity, constancy. *Lifestyle.* This concept is expressed in the following verses also:

*Be anxious for nothing, but **in everything** by prayer and supplication with thanksgiving let your requests be made known to God.*

Philippians 4:6

*With all prayer and petition pray **at all times** in the Spirit, and with this in view, be on the alert with all perseverance and petition for all the saints.*

Ephesians 6:18

*Now He was telling them a parable to show that **at all times** they ought to pray and not to lose heart.*

Luke 18:1

***Devote yourselves** to prayer, keeping alert in it with an attitude of thanksgiving.*

Colossians 4:2

*Epaphras, who is one of your number, a bondslave of Jesus Christ, sends you his greetings, **always laboring earnestly** for you in his prayers.*

Colossians 4:12

Without ceasing. In everything. At all times. Devotedly. Earnestly. This is how God wants us to communicate with Him. Certainly, corporate prayer is included, but "without ceasing" primarily involves two people—you and God. And therein lies the intimacy. Imagine one person in your life with whom you talked all the time, about everything. You would be *close.* If a period of time elapsed in which you had no contact, you would feel it. You would miss it. This connection is what gives you *life.*

Now, what if this person were God? What if you shared a daily intimacy like this with Him? It is our blessing as believers to have this kind of relationship with God. I am inconsistent with prayer journaling and war-rooming, but I can do one very simple thing, something you can do as well: Talk to God. Every day. All day.

The Lord is in my thoughts, tied to everything I do from the time I wake up. If I'm sluggish in the morning, I utter in my heart, *Lord, please refresh me, energize me by Your Spirit.* Or I may lay in bed for a moment, captivated by creation. *Lord, thank You for the mourning dove cooing outside my window.* As I brush my teeth, I talk to God about the day, asking Him to set my agenda, give me focus, shower me with grace for all that's ahead.

If I sense something bothering me from the day before, I ask, *What is this, Lord? Why is it on my mind? What do I need to do?* Sometimes it becomes clear that it's bothering me because I didn't handle things well. Maybe I said something I shouldn't have or I used the wrong tone. In this case, the Lord is graciously burdening me because I need to repent. So I pause, acknowledge the wrong, and ask the Lord to forgive me and then for help to rectify the wrong with the other person.

When I've got my coffee, I settle into my chair at the kitchen table with my Bible before me. This is my favorite time of day. Time set aside to quiet myself before God and pray. I love the example Jesus set in this: His days were hectic as He traveled, often surrounded by crowds, from one city to the next. But He would steal away to secluded places to pray (Mark 1:35). And if *He* felt prayer was a necessity, well . . .

This is also my set-aside time to study, over which I also pray—for understanding, for grace and strength to obey, for eyes to see people and situations as God does, for faith to believe. I often pray the very verses I'm studying, which I will delve into more below.

Many times, I'm convicted as the word pierces "as far as the division of soul and spirit, of both joints and marrow . . . to judge the thoughts and intentions of the heart" (Hebrews 4:12). I may move from tears to praise as I confess my sins before God and rejoice that His mercy endures forever.

Regular time in the Word is what fuels my prayers and keeps me in a praying mind-set. The Word of God is living and active and continues to work in our hearts and minds long after we've closed the Book and gone about our day. It shapes our words and our actions, guides our choices, and keeps our hearts lifted to God, to acknowledge and seek Him in all that arises.

Please don't take this as over the top or super spiritual. It just *happens*. As with every aspect of our Christian walk, "praying without ceasing" is God's grace at work, as He draws our thoughts toward Him. Remember—He wants us to talk to Him. And if Jesus calls us "friend" (John 15:15), there must be some way to tangibly experience that. He is Himself "the Word" (John 1:1), so staying in the Word and filling our thoughts with the Word enlivens the communication. Our lives become a living, breathing, ongoing dialogue with God. And there's so much to talk to Him about in the normal course of a day.

Cultivate a Heart of Gratitude and Praise

A simple and beautiful way to maintain a heart of prayer is to cultivate a heart of gratitude and praise to God. It's telling that "pray without ceasing" is sandwiched between two other key commands:

Rejoice always;
pray without ceasing;
in everything give thanks; for this is God's will for you in Christ Jesus.

1 Thessalonians 5:16–18

Prayer, praise, and thanks are a beautiful symphony. They complement and encourage one another. When prayer is a lifestyle, so too will be praise and gratitude. That's a powerful team! No matter what the issue, no matter how hard the challenge, prayer puts the focus on the Most High God. And when you're focused on God, you can't help but praise and give thanks. We see this dynamic in the book of Philippians as well:

*Rejoice in the Lord always; again I will say, **rejoice!** . . .*
*Be anxious for nothing, but in everything by **prayer** and supplication with **thanksgiving** let your requests be made known to God.*

Philippians 4:4, 6

Once again, prayer, praise, and thanks go hand in hand. With all three, our hearts are aimed squarely at God. In our gratitude, petitions, and praise, we are acknowledging Him, reveling in Him, living, moving, and breathing in Him. It is a life of continual worship unto Him.

When King David set up the tabernacle for worship, he appointed ministers specifically to thank and praise God:

Oh give thanks to the LORD, call upon His name;
Make known His deeds among the peoples.
Sing to Him, sing praises to Him;
Speak of all His wonders.
Glory in His holy name;
Let the heart of those who seek the LORD be glad.
Seek the LORD and His strength;
Seek His face continually.

1 Chronicles 16:8–11; Psalm 105:1–4

These verses intermingle the importance of prayer, thanks, and praise, even as they remind us to seek God *continually*. Though we may not see the answer to our prayers right away—or perhaps even in the way we wish to—our hearts will be glad as we seek Him.

We see the same heart of thanks and praise in the verses below. Notice what the people of God are thankful for:

Oh give thanks to the LORD, for He is good,
For His lovingkindness is everlasting.
Let the redeemed of the LORD say so,
Whom He has redeemed from the hand of the adversary
And gathered from the lands,
From the east and from the west,
From the north and from the south.

They wandered in the wilderness in a desert region;
They did not find a way to an inhabited city.
They were hungry and thirsty;
Their soul fainted within them.
Then they cried out to the LORD in their trouble;
He delivered them out of their distresses.
He led them also by a straight way,
To go to an inhabited city.
Let them give thanks to the LORD for His lovingkindness,
And for His wonders to the sons of men!
For He has satisfied the thirsty soul,
And the hungry soul He has filled with what is good.

Psalm 107:1–9

There is so much in those verses for which we too can continually thank and praise God. As believers, we also once wandered in the wilderness, so to speak. Our father was the devil (John 8:44), sin was our master, and as slaves, we "lived in the lusts of our flesh, indulging the desires of the flesh and of the mind" (Ephesians 2:3). From our den of darkness we couldn't see the light of the gospel because we were blind—and didn't even know we were blind. And had we known, there was no way to turn on the light or make ourselves see. Like the people of Israel, we hungered and thirsted and we turned to people and things that could not satisfy.

But because of the Lord's lovingkindness, we have been redeemed from the hand of the adversary. "[God] rescued us from the domain of darkness, and transferred us to the kingdom of His beloved Son" (Colossians 1:13). He saved us, not because of anything good we had done, but because of His mercy and grace. And because of Jesus, we need never hunger or thirst again (John 6:35).

We have "forever reasons" to give thanks and praise. No matter what we face, we are able to rejoice and give thanks because of the Lord's goodness and grace in redeeming us. We've been set free from the power of sin, and are no longer under condemnation. We have *now* blessings that stretch into eternity. We have current afflictions that couldn't possibly compare with the glory to come (2 Corinthians 4:17). Through Christ we are more than conquerors (Romans 8:37). As we meditate on the richness of our lives in Christ, gratitude and praise can't help but pour forth.

There are also abundant everyday reasons to praise and give thanks. The sun that rises and sets each day is a spectacular marvel, parading God's glory. Do you praise Him when you see it? Give thanks for the changing leaves of fall, the budding flowers of spring. The gentle breeze that caresses your face. The friend who thought of you at just the right time and called. The meal you just enjoyed. The sound of falling rain. The current trial you're facing—yes, give thanks even in that! And as I've heard the older saints say in their wisdom, thank Him because He woke you up this morning.

The more we notice even the "little things" for which we can give thanks and praise, the more we see God's goodness and grace at work in our lives. We begin to see His glory in all of creation, His kindness in the blessings that surround us, His love in the people He's put in our path. And every moment we thank God and praise Him, we are talking to Him. We are inviting Him into that moment of our day. We are realizing that He is in *every* moment of our day. Through it all, we are clinging to Him.

Pray When Your Flesh Rises

It happens every single day. We can count on it. There's a part of us that doesn't want to conform to the will of God, and it will rise up and rebel. I'm so glad the Bible lets us know what's going on:

For the flesh sets its desire against the Spirit, and the Spirit against the flesh; for these are in opposition to one another, so that you may not do the things that you please.

Galatians 5:17

The flesh is that part of us that hasn't been redeemed. It's our old nature, that which is well familiar with the course of this world and the momentary pleasures of sin—because we once were fully planted there. One day our entire selves will be gloriously redeemed, but until then, we have a daily battle on our hands.

Even the apostle Paul, who poured out his life for the sake of the gospel and was used mightily by God, battled his flesh. He said:

For I know that nothing good dwells in me, that is, in my flesh; for the willing is present in me, but the doing of the good is not. For the good that I want, I do not do, but I practice the very evil that I do not want. But if I am doing the very thing I do not want, I am no longer the one doing it, but sin which dwells in me.

Romans 7:18–20

We see it in countless moments. There are times when we encounter people who rub us the wrong way, or worse. Maybe a friend has said or done something hurtful. Your feelings rise up. You want nothing to do with this person, and you may even tell her so. You want others to know what she's done, so all can marvel at the injustice. And you might even contemplate ways to strike back, even if low-key.

Yet Jesus says we must love our enemies and pray for them. In God's economy, it's to one's glory to overlook an offense (Proverbs 19:11). And as believers our lives should be marked by forgiveness, kindness, and trusting God to vindicate wrongs.

We who are wives know there are times we don't want to submit to our husbands. Many of us struggle with this notion. Maybe in this one circumstance, you bristle. You don't agree with the direction your husband wants to take. Not that there's anything inherently wrong with it—it just doesn't make sense to you. Did he give it much thought? Did he pray about it? You feel compelled to tell him everything that's unwise about his choice, and why you can't get on board. Meanwhile, the Lord is saying, "as the church is subject to Christ, so also the wives ought to be to their husbands in everything" (Ephesians 5:24).

And what about that moment you're scrolling on social media and see your friend on vacation? Seems she's always blessed to be able to visit nice places. In fact, everything about her life seems blessed. She's even a gourmet cook and interior designer, always posting drool-worthy shots of dinner on her beautifully prepared table in her beautifully decorated kitchen. In five minutes flat, your mood has plummeted and you're discontent with your current season in life and all that you perceive is lacking.

Every such moment is a moment for which we can *pray*. The minute your feelings threaten to carry you in an unfruitful direction . . . the minute a thoughtful disagreement with your husband becomes an active stance in opposition . . . the minute you begin to feel envy and discontent . . . your flesh is rising up. We have to pray before it gets out of control.

That's the thing about the flesh: it wants the driver's seat, and it will actively seek the driver's seat. Moreover, the enemy uses our flesh to advance his schemes. If we give him a toehold, he will take a foothold—and more. That's why we are given cautions such as this: "Be angry, and yet do not sin; do not let the sun go down on your anger, and do not give the devil an opportunity" (Ephesians 4:26–27).

We are to be controlled by the Spirit, not the flesh (Galatians 5:16). It's not possible to please God in the flesh (Romans 8:8). Thus, I (and all of us) have the task of constantly putting my flesh to death, so that "it is no longer I who live, but Christ lives in me" (Galatians 2:20). This is not easy! We can put our flesh to death one minute and, with any number of possible provocations, it's resurrected the next. It's a battle we cannot win on our own. We need God's help.

The fact that our flesh rises up so often is something that can work for our good—if we allow it to keep us clinging to God through prayer. We will stay under the control of the Spirit as a result, and in sweet fellowship with our Lord.

Pray When You Need to Control Your Tongue

If you've wondered how you could possibly pray enough to make it a lifestyle—and if you're anything like me—this one tiny thing could keep you before the throne all day: the tongue. It's part of the flesh we talked about above, but it's *so* out of control, it deserves its own section.

Look how mischievous it is:

- It's a fire.
- It's a world of iniquity.
- It defiles the entire body.
- It sets on fire the course of our lives, and is set on fire by hell.
- No one can tame it.
- It's a restless evil.
- It's full of deadly poison.
- It blesses, and it curses.

And this is only from one chapter in the Bible (James 3). The book of Proverbs devotes dozens of verses to the tongue, many highlighting its perils:

- Death is in the power of the tongue (Proverbs 18:21).
- The tongue can pierce like the thrusts of a sword (Proverbs 12:18).
- The tongue can crush the spirit (Proverbs 15:4).

It's no wonder we are told to be quick to hear and slow to speak (James 1:19). We've got this fiery, untamable wonder inside of us, a weapon that can slice another person to bits in mere seconds. We feel a need to be heard, and even more, a need to be right. We react and overreact, opine and defend, grumble and complain—and we might even slip in a bit of gossip as we share someone's need for prayer. So often the better course is simply to keep quiet. But remember—that tongue is wild. We need the power of God to rein it in. We need prayer.

I get practice with this every day, right in my home. I don't know about you, but that's where I seem to be tested most. My husband and kids are the ones who see me in every mood under the sun. When I'm tired, stressed, hurried, or frustrated, my words too often reflect my emotional state. I can't count the number of times we've had a back-and-forth about something, and I feel the need to say *one last thing*, though I know I shouldn't—I pray even as I'm itching to say it.

Especially now that my children are older, I get a holy nudge more and more to be silent in those moments I feel a lecture on my tongue. Whatever I think I need to say, I've likely said before. And experience has told me that the repeat performance won't bode well. Still, my flesh is ready to press the point—so I'm thankful for God's grace in drawing me instead to cling to Him. It sounds something like this in my head: *Lord, You know there's so much I want to say right now, but You're prompting me to stay silent. Help me, Lord. Give me grace and strength to glorify You.*

The same dynamic is often at work in marriage. I don't want to be that contentious wife who drives her husband to a corner of the roof (Proverbs 21:9). When I bite my lip and pray, I've seen time and again how my husband may be won "without a word" (1 Peter 3:1–2). God is the only one who can work deep in another person's heart, and often our words hinder more than help. Staying quiet in a particular situation can do wonders.

But often we *are* called to speak. Death may be in the power of the tongue, but so is life (Proverbs 18:21). And though the tongue can cut like a sword, it can also bring healing (Proverbs 12:18). As we walk by the Spirit, our words should build up and give grace (Ephesians 4:29). God can use us to bring wisdom, peace, and blessing to any situation.

Like apples of gold in settings of silver
Is a word spoken in right circumstances.

Proverbs 25:11

In the midst of the circumstances of life, we can pray for that right word that will shine like gold. We can even pray for the right tone and the right heart to accompany that word. There's never a day when we don't need grace for our tongues—which means every day is an opportunity to cling as we pray that our words be pleasing.

Pray When Worry Hits

Absolutes in the Word of God always capture my attention. I marvel at this one: "Be anxious for nothing" (Philippians 4:6).

Nothing.

God is telling us that there is not a single thing about which we should worry. Ever.

Actually, God is *commanding* us not to worry.

Jesus spoke definitively of worry in His Sermon on the Mount:

- "Do not be worried about your life" (Matthew 6:25).
- "And who of you by being worried can add a single hour to his life?" (Matthew 6:27).
- "So do not worry about tomorrow; for tomorrow will care for itself" (Matthew 6:34).

We understand why God would tell us not to worry. He is the sovereign God of the universe. He commands each and every morning. He sets boundaries for the seas, telling them, "Thus far you shall come, but no farther" (Job 38:11). He dresses the lilies of the field and prepares food for the birds. Not one sparrow escapes His eye. How much more then is He watching over us, minding every matter that concerns us? He wants us to believe that this is so and to trust that it is so.

And we are grateful. We know that God has great love for us. We know that He is powerful and that He cares for His creation. We know, both from the pages of His Word and from the ways in which we have seen Him move in our own lives, that we have every reason to trust Him.

And yet, when we get the diagnosis . . . when our son or daughter rejects the faith . . . when there's sudden unemployment . . . when death strikes . . . it's hard to place that particular thing under the heading, "Be anxious for nothing." It's too big. Too unexpected. Too scary. Too beyond our control. Without trying, our minds grab hold of worry like a security blanket. Worry wakes us as we sleep, invades our minds as we drive or cook or shower. And it spirals, assuming facts that don't exist and adding speculation of worst-case scenarios.

Even in average, day-to-day matters, we are prone to worry. There's no end to the things that concern us about our loved ones—spouses, kids, parents, whoever. We have friends, coworkers, and neighbors on our hearts. We're balancing home and ministry, dogged by the feeling that we're not doing enough even as we juggle a thousand balls. And worry becomes one of those ever-present balls, always in the air, attached to each and every obligation.

But it accomplishes nothing, except to move us outside the will of God. And we'd probably all attest that we'd rather live without it. The best way to nix worry is to pray the moment it hits. No matter the issue, when worry begins to stir, go to God. He's given us promises, and He invites us to stand on them:

- Be anxious for nothing, but in everything by prayer and supplication with thanksgiving let your requests be made known to God. And the peace of God, which surpasses all comprehension, will guard your hearts and your minds in Christ Jesus (Philippians 4:6–7).
- Therefore humble yourselves under the mighty hand of God, that He may exalt you at the proper time, casting all your anxiety on Him, because He cares for you (1 Peter 5:6–7).
- "But seek first His kingdom and His righteousness, and all these things will be added to you" (Matthew 6:33).

I can't count the number of times I've prayed, *Lord, Your Word says for me to be anxious for nothing, so I have to believe You mean even this situation. I give you this care, Father, thankful that You are well able to handle it. I thank You also that You perfect the things that concern me, and that You will work this together for good. I praise You, Lord, for giving me peace I could never comprehend, peace that stands guard over my heart and mind in Christ.*

In that moment, nothing about the situation changes. The thing that caused worry still exists. But instead of clinging to worry, you're clinging to God. You're bringing Him front and center into the situation, allowing Him to permeate it with supernatural peace. In clinging to Him, you're reminded that nothing is too hard for Him, and that you can rest in His sovereign care of you.

We may not be able to stop worry from surfacing, but we don't have to let it linger and spiral. Praying and clinging manifest the power of God.

Listen to People's Hearts

Your husband mentions a challenging day ahead at work as he downs his orange juice and heads out the door. It sounded offhanded, but he seemed a little stressed. You braid your little girl's hair before school, and she frowns, says she hates her hair, something you've never heard her say. She wants it straight like Suzy's. Suzy's is prettier, she says. Then you find your son's NBA posters in the recycling bin. He didn't make the freshmen basketball team last week and now says he's done with sports altogether.

At home, in church and the workplace, and in conversations with everyone from close friends to the grocery store clerk, we hear people's hearts, since "the mouth speaks from that which fills [the] heart" (Luke 6:45). Often, people don't realize how much their words reveal. They're simply in the moment, maybe venting or telling a casual story. Maybe they're reacting to the situation around them. But as good listeners and observers, we can capture much to pray about.

For those of us with families, especially, this should be a way of life. Our ears should stay tuned to the messages our husbands and kids send—the things that excite them, or their moods, challenges, and disappointments. But perhaps their mood is the thing that challenges and disappoints *us*. Often, we hear things when we're all in rush-rush mode, when we don't have time to focus on details. But if we capture those moments and pray about what we're seeing and hearing, it makes all the difference—both for our loved ones and for us.

You can lift up your husband's concerns about his day, asking the Lord for an extra measure of grace, strength, wisdom, and favor. You can ask God for wisdom to know how to speak to your daughter's heart, and also ask Him to do a work in her heart, such that she sees the beauty of being made specially by Him, in His image. And as you retrieve your son's posters from the recycling bin, you can pray for the Lord to heal the hurt of disappointment, and to encourage him in the gifts and talents He's given. These prayers take mere minutes, and yet are packed with power.

This is true wherever we go. I remember once, at a family gathering, an older relative made a remark about the ethnicity of someone else's spouse. It was clear this family member did not approve of interracial marriage—so much so that she couldn't resist openly criticizing it, albeit in a room where the couple was not present. Though this family member professed to be a Christian, her words were tinged with prejudice and disdain. She had revealed her heart.

You've likely been in a similar situation. Maybe it didn't involve prejudice, but someone's heart was revealed in an unflattering way. We may be tempted to look down on those people, or find yet another room to talk about *them*. But with a heart lifted up to God, we understand that we've all got issues, lots of ugly stuff that the Lord has to root out. And, but for the grace of God, who knows where we'd be? So pray, right then, for the Lord to open that person's eyes to see her attitude as He sees it, to move her to sincere repentance, and to replace that heart attitude with one that glorifies Him.

One place many of us frequent, where hearts are consistently on display, is social media. Day and night, many of our friends and loved ones gather there, especially on Facebook. They celebrate, rant, opine, and affirm the opinions of others whose posts they share. And, through their posts and pictures, we gain insight into their hearts. We may see a heart that is distant from God or crying out for worth and attention. We may see brokenness, anger, or loneliness. Instead of mindlessly scrolling past—rolling our eyes at what we don't agree with, maybe being quick to comment in disagreement—we can pray.

As we actively listen to the hearts of others and pray for them, we are also clinging to God. In lifting up others, we're talking to Him, keeping our relationship with Him vibrant. And in turn, He will often speak to our hearts about how we can help the very people for whom we intercede.

Be Quick to Confess Sin

As we make prayer a lifestyle—and as we grow in our knowledge of God—we may find ourselves burdened more by sin. It's not necessarily that we are sinning more. But if our hearts are lifted up to God and our minds steadily renewed by the Word of God, we are more sensitive to sin. Whereas before, you may have been convicted by an unkind word you said to someone, now an unkind *thought* disturbs you. That's good news—it means you're growing. But watch for the enemy's schemes as he tries to twist this feeling.

We have to remember always that we are in a war. We belong to God and our eternity with Him is assured, but in the age-old battle between God and the devil, we are targets. "For our struggle is not against flesh and blood, but against the rulers, against the powers, against the world forces of this darkness, against the spiritual forces of wickedness in the heavenly places" (Ephesians 6:12). The devil schemes against us, and he will surely scheme to put distance between you and God—even as you purpose in your heart to cling.

One of Satan's favorite schemes is condemnation. When you sin, the enemy wants you to be burdened with guilt. He wants you to think you're now out of favor with God. He couldn't possibly love you, not after what you've done! Cling to God? No, you're not worthy.

But we have this powerful promise: "There is now no condemnation for those who are in Christ Jesus" (Romans 8:1). This means that every sin we commit—and given our flesh, sin is a daily occurrence—is under the blood of Jesus. The penalty has been paid.

The enemy knows this, of course. He knows you are sealed until the day of redemption (Ephesians 1:13–14), and there is no way he can steal your eternity with God. But he can attempt to disturb your present intimacy with God. Guilt over sin can cause you to separate yourself from God, much like Adam and Eve did in the Garden. But in Christ, we have the privilege of running *to* the throne of God, where there is an endless supply of grace and mercy.

In humility, we understand that we will say the wrong things, think the wrong things, do the wrong things—and even if we do the right things, it might be with the wrong motives. Pride alone can ensnare us in a million ways. But when we feel the gentle conviction of the Holy Spirit, we should simply be quick to confess the sin. This is a vital part of our prayer lives. Then we can thank and praise God that He is faithful and righteous to forgive us (1 John 1:9). We needn't carry the weight of guilt. It's over and done. Even when we sin, we can and should continue to cling.

We have talked about ways to make prayer a lifestyle. Daily, we can lift our hearts in gratitude and praise to God for blessings large and small, eternal and temporal. We can pray in the countless times our flesh rises and our tongues need to be checked and guided. We can pray when worry hits and as we listen to people's hearts. And we can pray when we are convicted of sin.

This list is in no way exhaustive. We should also pray when fear surfaces, and doubt and temptation. We should pray to know God's will in a given situation: *What would You have me to do, Lord? Which way should I go?* We should even pray for a heart to pray, for the Lord to be top of mind always. Talking to Him—about anything, any-where—should be the normal course of our days.

And in all of this, Scripture adds richness to our prayers. Praying Scripture is an excellent way to meditate on truth while also asking the Lord to establish that truth in our own lives and the lives of others. We have a promise from God that "if we ask anything according to His will, He hears us. And if we know that He hears us in whatever we ask, we know that we have the requests which we have asked from Him" (1 John 5:14–15). Praying the Word is praying God's will, and we can pray knowing that God hears us and will grant our request.

For example, we might grow distressed when we read, "love your enemies, do good to those who hate you, bless those who curse you, pray for those who mistreat you" (Luke 6:27–28). We think, *There's no way! How on earth could I ever do that?* And it's true. It *is* difficult, in our human flesh. But as believers we've been given the power of the Spirit, the power to live supernaturally. So we pray, *Lord, thank You for enabling me to walk by the Spirit. Help me to obey Your Word, to love my enemies, to do good to those who hate me, to bless those who curse me, and to pray for those who mistreat me.*

We might read the story of Mary and Martha and bemoan the fact that we are very much like Martha. We're the one who's caught up with busyness and worry and distraction more than the quietness of doing the "needful thing" of sitting at the Lord's feet (see Luke 10:38–42). But if we see this in ourselves, it's because the Lord has been gracious to show us. And it's not to leave us feeling bad about ourselves, but to bring us up higher. In those moments, we pray, *Lord, help me to prioritize sitting at Your feet and taking in Your Word, and to recognize when I am bothered and distracted with unnecessary things.*

And there are many verses of Scripture that are actually powerful prayers themselves. Here are a few of my favorites, ones that I have prayed for myself and countless others through the years, with the wording made personal:

- I pray, Father, that You would give me a spirit of wisdom and revelation in the knowledge of You. I pray that the eyes of my heart may be enlightened, so that I will know what is the hope of Your calling, what are the riches of the glory of Your inheritance in the saints, and what is the surpassing greatness of Your power toward me (Ephesians 1:17–19).

- Lord, I ask to be filled with the knowledge of Your will in all spiritual wisdom and understanding, so that I will walk in a manner worthy of You, to please You in all respects, bearing fruit in every good work and increasing in the knowledge of You; strengthened with all power according to Your glorious might, for the attaining of all steadfastness and patience, joyously giving thanks to You Father, who have qualified me to share in the inheritance of the saints in Light (Colossians 1:9–12).

- Lord, I pray that my love may abound still more and more in real knowledge and all discernment, so that I may approve the things that are excellent, in order to be sincere and blameless until the day of Christ; having been filled with the fruit of righteousness which comes through Jesus Christ, to Your glory and praise (Philippians 1:9–11).

- Lord, I pray to stand perfect and fully assured in all Your will (Colossians 4:12).

- Lord, I pray You direct my heart into Your love and the steadfastness of Christ. May You, the Lord of peace, continually grant me peace in every circumstance (2 Thessalonians 3:5, 16).

There are many other prayers in Scripture, especially in the Psalms, all of them rich for our souls, for our own hearts to lift back to God through prayer. The more we saturate our hearts with the Word of God, the more we will find ourselves praying the Word as a lifestyle.

We've covered a lot of ground in this chapter, but I hope you're left with the feeling that making prayer a lifestyle is not hard. Every day, there are situations in our lives that bring up natural reactions, impulses, and observations. Capturing these as prayer moments makes all the difference. Imagine clinging to God that way every day—nothing compares to an intimacy that sweet.

6

The Glue in Trials and Suffering

When we learned our first child would be a boy, my husband and I began talking about names in earnest, though the subject had been broached well beforehand. We had a running debate as to whether our son would be William Fleming Tate V. I could appreciate heritage and legacy, but how far did it need to go? Was this a line of kings? My husband could somewhat appreciate my sentiment, in theory. But once we learned for sure we were having a boy—well, 90 percent sure according to the ultrasound technician—a glimmer appeared in Bill's eye. Debate parameters shifted. "Should we call him 'Billy' or 'Will'?" he wanted to know.

One day after church, we lightheartedly mentioned the dilemma to our pastor. Amused, he hearkened back to the book of Acts, when the apostles drew lots to determine which of two men should replace Judas Iscariot. "Why don't you flip a coin?" our pastor said. Somehow, it seemed the exact thing to do.

We got our coin, agreeing that whoever lost would embrace the other's choice. I won, but my only choice had been "something else." Together we began brainstorming what that would be. I approached Bill sometime later with a possibility.

"How about Quentin?" I said.

Bill nodded slowly, in a way that told me the name was resonating. *Quentin*, derived from Latin, means "born fifth," preserving a bit of the family legacy while also infusing a bit of uniqueness. Bill liked it. God had given us the perfect solution.

When I think back on that time and our focus on the baby's name, I'm reminded of our mind-set as budding parents. The name meant something. We were casting a vision as to who our son would be, which is also true of the choice of his middle name—Emmanuel, which means "God with us."

And names weren't the only thing we pondered. We envisioned what this boy's life would consist of, the passions he would pursue. First and foremost we prayed that he would know and love the Lord, and live a life that glorifies Him. We talked about the schools he might attend, elementary through college. At the time, Bill was working at the University of Wisconsin. Maybe it would someday be, "Go, Badgers!"

Bill had played Little League baseball growing up and—from the time we met to this day—plays basketball weekly, so naturally sports was in view. And with one parent a lover of Venn diagrams and the other of sentence diagrams, we wondered whose academic genes he would inherit. All this while he was yet in the womb.

Wondering what would be was exciting. Our minds could delight in whatever we envisioned, and we certainly didn't envision difficulties. Sure, we'd have the terrible twos and the dreaded teen years to contend with, and life itself was fraught with the unexpected. But if there was such a thing as a typical upbringing with typical experiences and activities and circles of friends, that was what we envisioned for our son.

As I write this, Quentin will soon turn twenty—and I wouldn't exactly call his growing-up years "typical." He had social anxieties.

An old soul, he could easily talk to adults, but he had a hard time interacting with kids his own age. Very literally, he didn't know what to say, didn't know how to strike up a conversation. Besides, other boys were talking and playing sports—Quentin wanted nothing to do with sports. He was always deep in a book or a pile of Legos, creating his own imaginary world.

For years Quentin had hardly any friends. Bill and I would role-play with him, set up situations, give him words. We had him meet with counselors. We watched as years and years of situations unfolded, some difficult and heartbreaking. And we prayed. And prayed. And prayed. *Lord, You could easily send Quentin a friend. One friend, Lord. Why have You not answered?*

This is where I'm supposed to share the miraculous turnaround. The breakthrough. Suddenly Quentin came out of his shell and had a slew of friends! God is good!

And actually, we did see moments where God was undeniably at work, like the three summers Quentin went to a weeklong Christian camp, clearly outside of his comfort zone. One year, we showed up for closing ceremonies and were shocked to learn Quentin had been the talk of the talent show, as he'd wielded and juggled Wiffle ball bats as he did with his "light sabers" at home. And there was his internship at the Missouri History Museum, where he researched, wrote, and performed in historical plays. Once again, we were surprised to find that he had a solo, singing an old spiritual in a deep, melodic voice we hardly knew he had.

But many such experiences, things that we hoped were breakthroughs, were only momentary. In all of Quentin's growing-up years, he lacked a close friend to pal around with. It simply never happened.

I could look back on all those years and feel that God didn't answer our prayers. And actually, I *did* feel that way for a time. But with continued prayer and the grace of insight, I am grateful because He did answer in ways we could not have imagined. God *is* good. He used difficulties and trials to draw us closer to Him. In every situation, with every burden of my heart, I was before the throne. Whenever I didn't understand, whenever I grew weary, whenever I was frustrated with waiting, I was taking things up with God, telling Him how I felt—and that cultivated a closer relationship with Him. Sometimes there were only tears, and His presence would reassure me that He cared, that He loved our son more than we did, and that He was working beyond what we could see.

If life had been wonderfully easy, I wouldn't have learned to cling to God as I did. I wouldn't have been crying out to Him, drawing near, desperately keeping my eyes fixed on Jesus and not on circumstances. The difficulties were the glue that caused me to hold fast to the Lord. I *had* to cling. Clinging to God kept my mind on *Him*. It reminded me that God is faithful, and that He's sovereign. I could trust Him. Clinging to God gave unsurpassing peace and joy.

And in the midst of these difficulties, God drew someone else to cling to Him—Quentin. He'd always had a heart for God, and I noticed in his teen years that that relationship was deepening. He was talking about God more and more and reading the Bible more and more. I would go to his room late at night and see books spread out as he studied the Scriptures.

Then one day he casually mentioned that Jesus was his closest friend. This momma's heart melted. All the years of praying for the Lord to send him a friend, and the Lord answered with Himself. *He* would be Quentin's close friend. The Lord drew our son through his hardships and used his hardships to cultivate an intimate relationship with Him. He taught Quentin to cling. Never would I have imagined such a gracious gift.

Our story isn't unique. God uses trials and hardships to draw all of us closer. Often we would rather do without the struggle, but it's the struggle that moves us to know Him in a deeper way. In the Bible, David certainly found this to be true. Earlier, we looked at events in his life that reveal God's ways. Let's look at those same events from the standpoint of what they taught David.

David's Trials Taught Him to Cling

I highly doubt David wanted to fight animals as ferocious as a bear or lion. He would have preferred that they simply keep away from his sheep—that he and the predators just avoid one another. But David wasn't so fortunate—those ferocious animals would make their way among the flock and try to steal his lambs. And when they did, David was immediately caught in a struggle, perhaps internally at first: Would he really go after them? Would he really risk his life?

He did go after them, and he rescued the lambs from the very mouth of both the lion and the bear, killing them when they rose up against him (1 Samuel 17:35). But David knew that it was God who ultimately had delivered him from those beasts. He was looking to God, no doubt praying to God. Those trials taught David to trust God, to cling to Him in the midst of adversity.

And what about that time when David, still a shepherd boy, was told by his father to take lunch to his three oldest brothers, at war with the Philistines? For David it was an ordinary day, and the task was simple. He could not have anticipated any difficulties. He would drop off the food, see how his brothers were faring, and bring back word to his father.

But when he got to the army's camp and heard Goliath's challenge— and saw all of Israel's fighting men fleeing in fear—David knew they were in trouble. Like it or not, he was thrown into another very real struggle. If he did nothing, he and his people would be slaves to the Philistines.

But David's mind went immediately to his God. That's what cling-ing does: it keeps God top of mind. Rather than despair, fear, and give up hope, David saw this hardship as another opportunity to hold fast to God. If he could cling to God in a struggle with a lion, why not with a fearsome giant?

Still, David was facing the biggest trial of his life. Goliath was more than nine feet tall, and "he wore a bronze helmet, and his bronze coat of mail weighed 125 pounds. He also wore bronze leg armor, and he carried a bronze javelin on his shoulder. The shaft of his spear was as heavy and thick as a weaver's beam, tipped with an iron spearhead that weighed 15 pounds" (1 Samuel 17:5–7 NLT). David, on the other hand, had no armor (he had rejected Saul's), and his weapon of choice was a sling and five stones. The circumstances were dire, but that's what caused David to cling all the more.

In dire circumstances, we are faced with the stark reality that we have no strength in ourselves. No personal resources. No clever strategies. There's absolutely nothing we can do. We *have* to cling to God—we have to, that is, if we want to hold onto hope. And that's what David did. He ran to that battle line clinging to God, knowing that God would fight for him. And God did. It was a stunning victory, with the battle over in mere seconds as that single stone to the forehead felled the giant.

But David would learn that not all struggles end so quickly. Some must be walked out for weeks or months or years, which deepens our relationship with God as we cling through troubled times. Such was the case with David's extended hardship with King Saul.

Hardships can seem so unfair. David had met the test of his life, and he'd trusted God. He had to have thought his troubles were over when the giant hit the ground. Yet they were only just beginning. Killing the giant won David many admirers—too many. King Saul burned with envy and soon made it his mission to kill David.

Think about this. Even before the battle with Goliath, David had been anointed the next king of Israel. It was a very real promise from God. Yet there was no timeline given as to *when* he would become king. Now, the current king was seeking to end David's life. It was a trial of epic proportion. Not only was David's life at risk by his own king, but his faith was also being tested. What would become of his relationship with God? Would he grow bitter and distance himself from God? Or would he continue to cling?

David lets us know, through his psalms particularly, that the intense, years-long hardship of running from Saul caused him to dwell more intimately with God. It was when David was depleted, when his soul was dry and weary, that he learned to seek God earnestly (Psalm 63:1). When his life hung by a thread, he learned to meditate on God's goodness, and to be satisfied not with a miraculous change of circumstance but with God Himself (verses 4–7). David learned that clinging is two-sided—"My soul clings to You; Your right hand upholds me" (verse 8). How powerful, this idea of God upholding us during times of trial as we cling to Him.

David's trials taught him how *personal* God is, and he shared that truth in Psalm 18. It's one of my favorites for that very reason. I cling to the first three verses when I especially need to cling to God during hardship.

"I love You, O LORD, my strength."
The LORD is my rock and my fortress and my deliverer,
My God, my rock in whom I take refuge;
My shield and the horn of my salvation, my stronghold.
I call upon the LORD, who is worthy to be praised,
And I am saved from my enemies.

The intimacy in the first verse alone is amazing. David the warrior, the giant slayer, the anointed king—professing his love to almighty God. That intimacy was forged through the wilderness of adversity. No one had to tell David in theory that God is a rock, a fortress, a deliverer, a shield, or a stronghold. It wasn't just nice information to store inside a database of knowledge. David *needed* God to be those things to him. When the storm was raging, David *needed* God to be his refuge in the ongoing trials he endured. He describes them as "cords of death" and "torrents of ungodliness" (Psalm 18:4) that surrounded and terrified him. But he didn't attempt to weather them alone, nor did he cave in despair. "In my distress I called upon the LORD, and cried to my God for help" (verse 6). David, again, was clinging to God. As a result, he could say that God is:

My strength.
My rock.
My fortress.

My deliverer.

My shield.

The horn of *my* salvation.

My stronghold.

Each of these attributes of God was proven in a profoundly personal way to David. Yet that wasn't because David had been anointed king or because he possessed some special quality that God favored. It was because David chose to cling to God in the midst of adversity. And the same can be true for us. When we run to God and cry out to Him in our times of need, we are able to behold God at work as our own fortress, our own stronghold, our own rock, and our own strength. We see Him in ways we cannot otherwise see Him.

When there's no affliction, we don't need a shield. When days are rosy, we don't need a hiding place. But when the storm is raging and you don't know how you'll make it from one moment to the next without losing your mind, you cling to God with everything in you—that's when you experience that divine fortress. By anyone's measure, you should be crushed, but the circumstances aren't touching you. You're protected. Instead of losing your mind, you've got peace of mind. Instead of caving, you're abounding. You're learning the greatness of God's power. You're even learning the tenderness of His compassion. Like David, you are awed as you say, "I love You, O Lord, my strength."

I have memorized and meditated on these three verses, uttering them even through tears. We don't need to pretend that trials are a light matter. They are many-faceted and can be downright *hard*. But we never need endure them apart from God. Let them be the glue that causes you to cling like never before.

Job's Suffering Moved Him to Cling More Deeply

In the midst of trials, suffering, and disappointment, one of our biggest questions is *Why?* Why is this happening? Why am I—or why is my loved one—going through this? We want to somehow make sense of things. We need to measure the reason and the purpose against the pain and the heartache. We need to understand.

David knew why he was on the run, sort of. He knew that King Saul wanted him dead, and he likely knew that jealousy played a part—David's success as a warrior had people singing, "Saul has slain his thousands, and David his ten thousands" (1 Samuel 18:7). Still, David was perplexed because he'd done nothing wrong. In fact, he'd ministered to Saul by playing the harp for him, married Saul's daughter, and served Saul well as a soldier. Yet David found himself escaping through his own bedroom window as Saul's men came after him. David asked Jonathan, Saul's son, "What have I done? What is my iniquity? And what is my sin before your father, that he is seeking my life?" (1 Samuel 20:1).

What David didn't know was that much of Saul's issue was spiritual. Saul had disobeyed a direct command from God, causing God to reject Saul as king. The Spirit of God had departed from Saul, and an evil spirit terrorized him thereafter (1 Samuel 16:14), inciting irrational and murderous behavior. David feared for his life for years without a full understanding as to why. Yet he came to understand what was most needful—to cling to God in the midst.

In that respect, Job's experience was similar. Most of the book of Job deals with speculation as to why he was suffering. Why did he lose all of his possessions and all ten of his children in one day? And if that weren't enough, why was he then struck with painful boils from head to toe, such that he sat unrecognizable among the ashes? Job's three friends contended that his circumstances were judgment for sin. If Job would only seek God, put away iniquity, and repent, one said, "Your life would be brighter than noonday" (Job 11:17).

But Job knew it wasn't that simple. He had no known sin in his life, which made his plight all the more incomprehensible. Still, he was willing to ask God, "Have I sinned? What have I done to You, O watcher of men? Why have you set me as Your target?" (Job 7:20).

Perhaps that was the most painful aspect to endure, this thought that God had set Himself against Job. "For the arrows of the Almighty are within me, their poison my spirit drinks," Job said. "The terrors of God are arrayed against me" (Job 6:4).

Job could only see the earthly dynamic. He didn't know the spiritual dynamic at work, one that had originated before the very throne of God. A remarkable scene had taken place on a day when the angelic host had come to present themselves before God. The fallen angel, Satan, had appeared with them. When God asked where he'd come from, Satan answered, "From roaming about on the earth and walking around on it" (Job 1:7).

Then God said something astounding: "Have you considered My servant Job? For there is no one like him on the earth, a blameless and upright man, fearing God and turning away from evil" (1:8). God *knew* Job, intimately. He knew Job's ways, his heart, his dedication, and his faithfulness. He called Job "*My* servant." What God had with Job was personal.

Of course, Satan already knew these things about Job. The devil roams the earth not for idle amusement but to seek whom he can destroy (1 Peter 5:8). And Job's faithfulness to God had surely made him an enemy of Satan. But Satan couldn't get to Job because of God's protection. The devil said to God, "Have you not made a hedge about him and his house and all that he has, on every side?" (Job 1:10). Satan challenged God: "But put forth Your hand now and touch all that he has; he will surely curse You to Your face" (1:11).

God allowed Satan to touch Job's possessions, but he couldn't touch Job himself. Don't miss the fact that it was God who set the parameters—He's *always* in control. In a single day, the enemy took Job's possessions and caused a great wind to strike the house in which his sons and daughters were feasting. The house collapsed, and all ten of them died. When Job heard what had happened, he mourned. But he also worshipped, saying, "The LORD gave and the LORD has taken away. Blessed be the name of the LORD" (1:21).

Satan was no doubt seething because of Job's worshipful attitude. He showed up again before the throne of God, ready to up the ante. This time Satan wanted permission to do what he couldn't do before—touch Job's flesh. *That* would cause Job to curse God to His face, he said. God allowed it, providing that the enemy spare Job's life. So Satan "smote Job with sore boils from the sole of his foot to the crown of his head" (2:7). And the enemy waited. He just knew that suffering like this would cause Job to turn his back on God.

Job indeed took issue with God. He questioned and challenged God, and called Him to account for what seemed grossly unjust. But Job did not turn his back on God. Remarkably, he said,

"But it is still my consolation,
And I rejoice in unsparing pain,
That I have not denied the words of the Holy One."

Job 6:10

And *this*:

"My foot has held fast to His path;
I have kept His way and not turned aside.
I have not departed from the command of His lips;
I have treasured the words of His mouth more than my necessary food."

Job 23:11–12

Job used "clinging" language. His foot *held fast* to God's path and God's way, not turning aside. As we discussed in earlier chapters, this includes holding fast to God's Word, which Job declared as well. He treasured God's words. He couldn't deny them, despite the searing pain he endured from one moment to the next. Not only was he consoled by this, but he could rejoice in it as well.

What's more, even in his questioning and challenging, Job often talked directly to God, as here:

"Your hands fashioned and made me altogether,
And would You destroy me?
Remember now, that You have made me as clay;
And would You turn me into dust again?"

Job 10:8–9

And here Job speaks to God from the anguish in his heart:

"I cry out to You for help, but You do not answer me;
I stand up, and You turn Your attention against me.
You have become cruel to me;
With the might of Your hand You persecute me.
You lift me up to the wind and cause me to ride;
And You dissolve me in a storm."

Job 30:20–22

In all of this, Job does not curse God. He does not renounce his faith or sever ties to the Almighty. Rather, Job expresses the human pain that many of us have felt: of crying out to God and hearing nothing but silence, feeling nothing but rejection. Clinging to God doesn't prevent our being raw with Him, being honest about our disappointment and frustrations. When we do so, we are *drawing near* to God. Rather than shutting down, we are communicating with Him.

In Job's suffering, though, he went beyond disappointment and frustration to presumption. In making his case of innocence, Job essentially found fault with God, as if God had done him wrong. "If I have walked with falsehood, and my foot has hastened after deceit," Job complained, "let Him weigh me with accurate scales, and let God know my integrity" (31:5–6). Job presumed to know better than God what his lot in life should be, and even presumed unfairness on God's part. If he were weighed with accurate scales, he claimed, then he wouldn't be in his current predicament. And though we empathize—who can begin to imagine that great weight of suffering and how we might respond?—we learn much from God when He finally responded to Job.

After His silence for much of the book, God "answered Job out of the whirlwind" (38:1) in more than one hundred twenty verses. Trust me. These are verses to read and re-read often. There's something about God Himself speaking in first person. There's nothing like it. The power. The sovereignty. The majesty. The jaw-dropping *awe*.

God primarily asked questions, aimed at one overarching theme. He wanted to know if Job had even a fraction of God's knowledge and wisdom, enough to presume to question God or judge Him as unfair. Those questions are as blistering as they are inspiring. Here is a sample:

> *"Where were you when I laid the foundation of the earth?*
> *Tell Me, if you have understanding,*
> *Who set its measurements? Since you know."*

Job 38:4–5

> *"Who enclosed the sea with doors*
> *When, bursting forth, it went out from the womb;*
> *When I made a cloud its garment*
> *And thick darkness its swaddling band,*
> *And I placed boundaries on it*
> *And set a bolt and doors,*
> *And I said, 'Thus far you shall come, but no farther;*
> *And here shall your proud waves stop'?"*

Job 38:8–11

> *"Have you ever in your life commanded the morning,*
> *And caused the dawn to know its place . . . ?"*

Job 38:12

> *"Who prepares for the raven its nourishment*
> *When its young cry to God*
> *And wander about without food?"*

Job 38:41

Can we just pause here for a second? Although this is styled as a rebuke, does it not make you want to shout with joy? This is the God we cling to! Our God is the Most High God, who commands the morning and sets boundaries for the seas, and yet who is compassionate to feed the birds of the sky. And we know that if His eye is on the sparrow, He is watching over us intently.

In the midst of His majestic discourse, God stops to ask Job, "Will the faultfinder contend with the Almighty? Let him who reproves God answer it" (40:2). Imagine how you might respond. Who *could* respond, with much more than a humble gulp? Unsurprisingly, Job admits he has no reply, other than the obvious: "Behold, I am insignificant" (40:4). And with that, God continues to break down His might and omniscience for two more chapters, until Job declares finally what he *does* know:

> *"I know that You can do all things,*
> *And that no purpose of Yours can be thwarted. . . .*
> *Therefore I have declared that which I did not understand,*
> *Things too wonderful for me, which I did not know. . . .*
> *I have heard of You by the hearing of the ear;*
> *But now my eye sees You;*
> *Therefore I retract,*
> *And I repent in dust and ashes."*

Job 42:2–3, 5–6

In His grace and kindness, God put His sovereignty on magnificent display. How could Job possibly know the millions of things God orders in the universe, let alone understand or begin to run them himself? How could he presume even to understand what was happening in his own life? God had already declared Job blameless and upright, yet Job was not perfect. He needed a greater understanding of who God is—and who Job was not. As a result, Job could cling to God all the more, not because he understood the "why" of his suffering, but because He better understood the sovereignty of God.

It's not easy to read the book of Job. We shudder to think that a suffering as awful as Job's could ever approach our doorstep. And, if we're honest, we just plain wish God wouldn't be in the business of "recommending" His faithful servants to the enemy. For many, the best part of the book is the final chapter, when God restores Job's fortune and his family. But the entire book is a great blessing for those who desire to cling to God in the midst of suffering.

Job's story tells us that there's much more at work than we can see. It reminds us that if we're under spiritual attack, it's only because God allowed it—and He remains in control. It drives home the fact that people are not the ones we cling to—they don't understand why we're going through what we're going through (even as we ourselves don't) and ultimately can't do anything about it. Only God can. And Job's story gives us, in God's own voice, glorious truths about God to cling to—truths which build our faith and trust. We should keep all of these truths close, since suffering is part of the life of every believer.

Suffering Well for Christ's Sake

That sounds weird, doesn't it? We hardly want to acknowledge suffering as a possibility in our lives, so what is this about suffering *well*? David, Job, and countless others in the Bible endured trials and suffering according to the will of God. And suffering is also part of our lives as believers. In fact, we are called to suffer for the sake of Christ.

> *For to you it has been granted for Christ's sake, not only to believe in Him, but also to suffer for His sake.*
>
> Philippians 1:29

> *For you have been called for this purpose, since Christ also suffered for you, leaving you an example for you to follow in His steps.*
>
> 1 Peter 2:21

Jesus is the reason we are called to suffer, as well as our example in suffering. He is eternal God, existing in glory before time began, and yet He humbled Himself by putting on human flesh and walking the earth as a man. He committed no sin, yet was sentenced to the most brutal death—death on a cross. As sinful men spit on Him and mocked, slapped, and scourged Him, He could have asserted His divinity. He could have called legions of angels to His aid. Instead, Jesus was silent, enduring the suffering, "entrusting Himself to Him who judges righteously" (1 Peter 2:23). In Jesus's suffering, it was our sins He bore on the cross, "so that we might die to sin and live to righteousness" (2:24)—so that we might be healed.

Now, as believers in Christ, we are called to patiently endure suffering for His sake. This is the kind of suffering that comes from doing what is right, from pursuing Christlikeness. We may lose friends because of our relationship with Jesus, suffer rejection from coworkers or neighbors because of Jesus, maybe even lose jobs because we choose to walk in integrity.

Even more painful, many have endured rejection from spouses, children, and parents, among others, because of commitment to Christ. Jesus Himself told us this could happen when He said, "Do not think that I came to bring peace on the earth; I did not come to bring peace, but a sword. For I came to set a man against his father, and a daughter against her mother . . . and a man's enemies will be the members of his household" (Matthew 10:34–36). That's the cost of taking up our cross and following Jesus. We gain priceless treasure in Him, but suffering is an indispensable part of the equation.

Of course, as we learn from the book of Job, the enemy is behind much of our suffering. The devil is still roaming the earth, as he did in Job's day—all the way back to the time of Adam and Eve. He "prowls around like a roaring lion, seeking someone to devour" (1 Peter 5:8). And he's got a whole host of demons with him: "For our struggle is not against flesh and blood, but against the rulers, against the powers, against the world forces of this darkness, against the spiritual forces of wickedness in the heavenly places" (Ephesians 6:12). The enemy is never short on schemes against us. He tempts, accuses, inflicts, incites, and shoots flaming arrows designed to render us ineffective in glorifying Christ.

How do we not only endure all of this, but endure it well?

We cling to our Lord and Savior. The one who endured suffering on our behalf gives us abundant grace, strength, and protection in the midst of all He calls us to endure for His sake. We cling by remembering and following His example. Meditating on the cross strengthens us and builds our faith. If Jesus could humbly and patiently endure suffering, by grace we can as well. We owe Him our very lives; suffering for His sake is a small price to pay in comparison to all He has done for us.

We cling by praying in the midst of adversity. We aren't called to suffer alone or in our own strength. We run to the throne of grace whenever we have need, and we especially need God in times of trial and suffering. Prayer gives us divine insight and focus, eternal perspective, increased peace and joy, and strength to abound. Prayer is also part of the armor of God we've been given. We cling by standing firm in that armor—the belt of truth, the breastplate of righteousness, shoes of peace, the shield of faith, the helmet of salvation, and the sword of the Spirit, which is the word of God—all of which protect us against the enemy's arrows and schemes (Ephesians 6:11–18).

I love this promise: "After you have suffered for a little while, the God of all grace, who called you to His eternal glory in Christ, will Himself perfect, confirm, strengthen and establish you" (1 Peter 5:10). God also encourages us with the truth that if we suffer for the name of Christ, we are *blessed* and should even rejoice (1 Peter 4:13–14). It's a high calling, a privilege, to be named with our Lord and Savior. Whatever we experience here on earth will not compare to the glories to come.

Moreover, God uses trials in our lives to *teach* us to endure during our stay on earth. These verses run often through my mind:

Consider it all joy, my brethren, when you encounter various trials, knowing that the testing of your faith produces endurance. And let endurance have its perfect result, so that you may be perfect and complete, lacking in nothing.

James 1:2–4

Did you notice it doesn't say *if* but *when* you encounter various trials? Trials will come, of infinite variety, shape, and color. It's what we do in the midst of trials that makes the difference. When we understand that trials are a faith test, that God is using them to produce endurance which ultimately leads to perfection, we can consider it all joy. I know it sounds odd to consider trials joy, but clinging to God helps us to keep this godly perspective.

As you read this book, you are likely enduring some form of trial or suffering, or perhaps you have recently been through such a season. It may be a personal crisis, or one involving a loved one. It may involve loss, heartbreak, rejection, betrayal, sickness, or pain. Such seasons are *hard*, and often we cannot see an end to them. But it is my prayer that you will see each hardship in your life as an opportunity to cling more fiercely to the Lord.

Cry out to God. Weep in His loving presence. Feast long on His Word. Stand on His promises. Worship His goodness. Praise His sovereignty. Trust that He sees you, that He loves you, and that He cares for you beyond what you can imagine. Rather than focus on the circumstance, focus on the Lord. Let Him be the very center of your existence—when your mind is stayed on Him, He keeps you in perfect peace (Isaiah 26:3).

Is any of this easy? Honestly, no. Trials and suffering can loom like dreadful mountains, ever drawing our gaze, causing us to tremble. And the enemy of our souls works to move our focus away from a sovereign God and onto doubt and fear. But this is why we cling *daily*. We choose intimacy with God every day, spending time in His presence, enjoying regular conversation. When our gaze begins to drift, we ask Him for focus. When fear begins to rise, we ask Him to exchange it for peace. When we feel He's not hearing us or even walking with us, we cling still—because we walk by faith, not by sight. We hold fast to our living hope. We marvel that despite the storm, there's praise in our spirit and joy on our lips because the Lord is our help. Like David in his time of trial, we say:

My soul clings to You;
Your right hand upholds me.

Psalm 63:8

7

The Wedge of Disobedience

David was finally king over all Israel. He'd been anointed as king while still a shepherd boy, the youngest and least likely among his father's eight sons. He had proven his courage and his zeal for the glory of God by fighting and ultimately defeating the Philistine giant Goliath. His fame as a great warrior, fearless in battle against Israel's enemies, had spread. But his own king, jealous over David's success, had issued a death sentence against him. David was forced to flee his home and spend years on the run, hiding in the wilderness, fearing for his life.

The most trying years of his life became years of deep intimacy-building with God. David *clung* to God. It was during this season that he wrote of waiting on God, finding refuge in God, crying out in sorrow to God, being hidden in God, and gaining satisfaction in God. From his nearness to God, he could proclaim, "I love You, O LORD, my strength" (Psalm 18:1) and praise God as his rock, fortress, deliverer, refuge, shield, stronghold, horn of his salvation—as his God (18:2–3).

David was so close to God that he had an especially tender conscience. When King Saul, on the hunt for David, stopped in a cave to relieve himself, he unknowingly came within inches of the man he'd declared his enemy. David's men saw an opportunity for him to kill Saul, putting an end to the madness of life on the run. But when David secretly cut off the edge of Saul's robe, his conscience was pricked. As king, Saul was God's anointed—and David would trust God for deliverance in His time.

After more than four years, God did deliver David. Saul was killed in battle, and God's promise soon came to pass—David was established as king over Israel. The man with a heart to cling to God was now on the throne, and he still had a zeal for God. One of David's first acts was to bring the ark of God into Jerusalem, where he'd made his home. After a tragic accident that delayed the move for three months (see 2 Samuel 6:6–11), the ark was brought to Jerusalem and the celebration was amazing.

With shouting and trumpets blowing before the ark, David was so excited that he "was dancing before the LORD with all his might" (2 Samuel 6:14). With all his might! Picture that scene. David was beside himself that the presence of God would take up residence in the city, near him. God was enthroned not just in the ark but in David's heart. As he danced, his heart overflowed with praise—because of his intimacy with God.

Yet the Bible signals a change in David's life, seven to ten years later, with these words: "Then it happened in the spring, at the time when kings go out to battle, that David sent Joab and his servants with him and all Israel. . . . But David stayed at Jerusalem" (2 Samuel 11:1).

We are given the standard: kings lead their troops in battle. That's what they do. And we know, especially, that that's what David had done. The famed warrior was known for seeking God in battle and himself leading the charge. But this time, David sent his men to battle while he stayed home. The Bible doesn't give us the reason why, but it signals what we need to know—something was off. We know this as well: the devil prowls around looking for someone to devour.

One evening, out for a walk on the flat roof of his palace, David saw a beautiful neighbor woman bathing—and he asked about her. David was told her name, Bathsheba, and that she was the wife of a man named Uriah, called "the Hittite."

David—the man who had prayed, "Make me know Your ways, O Lord; teach me Your paths. Lead me in Your truth and teach me" (Psalm 25:4–5)—knew God's truth about adultery. "Thou shalt not commit adultery" was a commandment handed down from Moses. Adultery was sin.

Though David always ran to God when he was a hair's breadth from death, he didn't run to God in the face of this temptation. He didn't cry for help. Didn't ask that God be a refuge from his raging flesh, a deliverer from the lust of his eyes. In a pivotal moment, David *didn't* cling to God at all. Instead, he sent messengers to call the woman to him, and he slept with her. Before long, David got word from Bathsheba: "I am pregnant" (2 Samuel 11:5).

Here was another opportunity to cling. David could have prayed, *Lord, I have sinned against You. I ask You to forgive me. I'm in a terrible bind, Lord. Show me what to do. I understand I have to deal with the consequences. Help me to walk uprightly from this moment forth.* But David didn't look to God. He took matters into his own hands.

The king sent for Bathsheba's husband, Uriah, to return home from the war. David's plan was for Uriah to sleep with his wife, so that the baby could be passed off as his—but Uriah wouldn't go home. An honorable man, he refused to enjoy time with his wife while his fellow soldiers were away at battle.

So David enacted Plan B. He told his commander to put Uriah on the front lines of battle, and then withdraw from him. Uriah was killed by the Ammonites, according to plan. After Bathsheba's time of mourning, David took her as his wife, and they had a son.

And God was watching it all. "The thing that David had done was evil in the sight of the Lord" (2 Samuel 11:27).

We Need to See Sin as God Sees It

We live in a grace-saturated Christian culture. Believers are well versed, as we should be, in the truth that it is by grace that we are saved, through faith (Ephesians 2:8). Many believers have a healthy assurance of salvation, knowing that nothing can separate us from the love of God which is in Christ Jesus (Romans 8:39). As we live out our Christian lives, we are reminded that God's grace is available for all that we do, despite all that we do, continually.

And these are precious truths. But if we are not careful, we can begin to take a light view of sin. We can think that it almost doesn't matter. If we sin, God is gracious to forgive—so no big deal, right? Yet sin is a very big deal to God. His response to David is sobering and instructive for us today.

God sent a prophet to David. Nathan had counseled David in the past and was a trusted man of God. He told David a parable about a rich man and a poor man. The rich man had many flocks and herds, but the poor man had only one little ewe lamb, which he cherished. When a traveler visited the rich man, he didn't take an animal from his own flock. Instead, the rich man took the poor man's ewe lamb and prepared it for the traveler.

David's ire rose immediately. The man needed to be put to death! He would pay restitution fourfold!

Notice the tactic God used through Nathan. David needed to be struck by the ugliness of his sin, but he was too close, perhaps too enamored with Bathsheba, to see it. An illustration drove home the horror of the situation.

David must have been stunned by Nathan's words: "You are the man!" (2 Samuel 12:7). The prophet continued:

> *"Thus says the Lord God of Israel, 'It is I who anointed you king over Israel and it is I who delivered you from the hand of Saul. I also gave you your master's house and your master's wives into your care, and I gave you the house of Israel and Judah; and if that had been too little, I would have added to you many more things like these!"*

> 2 Samuel 12:7–8

David's sin was a personal affront to God. God had chosen David and delivered him. He had blessed David abundantly. Was it not enough? Was David not grateful and content with all that God had done for him? In His goodness, God would have given more.

Do we see our own sin from this standpoint? As believers, we have been chosen and delivered by God as well. We are blessed with every spiritual blessing, and also with material blessings. Imagine how God feels as our sin reflects an attitude of discontentment and ingratitude with what He has given.

God had more to say:

> *"Why have you despised the word of the LORD by doing evil in His sight? You have struck down Uriah the Hittite with the sword, have taken his wife to be your wife, and have killed him with the sword of the sons of Ammon. Now therefore, the sword shall never depart from your house, because you have despised Me and have taken the wife of Uriah the Hittite to be your wife."*
>
> 2 Samuel 12:9–10

The words in bold show once more how *personal* this is to God. In his sin, David had not only despised the word of God, he had despised *God*. I doubt David was thinking about God when he sent for Bathsheba, or later, when he gave word for her husband to be killed in battle. He was thinking about his own pleasure, and then how to cover it up. But whatever may be in our own minds as we sin, it's God's mind that matters. What *He* thinks is key. And from God's standpoint, sin reveals a heart that despises Him and His Word.

When David heard God's words, as well as what his judgment would be, he responded: "I have sinned against the LORD." Nathan replied, "The LORD also has taken away your sin" (2 Samuel 12:13). Sin had caused David to turn for a time from the God he loved. In exchange for intimacy with Bathsheba, he had forsaken intimacy with God—a disastrous trade. But in acknowledging his sin, David turned heavenward. Once again, he was choosing intimacy with his God.

Sin Affects Our Intimacy with God

We cling to God by prayer, through knowing Him through His Word, and by faith and trust in the midst of trials. We also cling through our obedience to God. Being in God's will causes us to dwell closely with Him. Conversely, sin puts a wedge between us and God.

We saw this with Adam and Eve. They enjoyed close fellowship with God until the moment they sinned. Then, suddenly, there was distance, beginning in their hearts. When Adam and Eve heard God walking in the garden, they couldn't bear to be in His presence, so they hid from Him. Ultimately, they were sent out of the garden, their sin having caused a permanent separation between themselves and God.

David, who had written much about intimacy with God, described how sin affected that intimacy. He said:

When I kept silent about my sin, my body wasted away
Through my groaning all day long.
For day and night Your hand was heavy upon me;
My vitality was drained away as with the fever heat of summer.

Psalm 32:3–4

David groaned often when he was on the run from Saul, but he was groaning to God. He was clinging to God. And despite his groaning, he could experience joy and satisfaction in the Lord. But when David was in sin, unrepentant, he placed himself against God. And the impact was disastrous to his soul. Rather than abounding in God's strength, sin drained him.

Now, as David acknowledged, "Against You, You only, I have sinned and done what is evil in Your sight" (Psalm 51:4), he pleaded:

Create in me a clean heart, O God,
And renew a steadfast spirit within me.
Do not cast me away from Your presence
And do not take Your Holy Spirit from me.

Restore to me the joy of Your salvation
And sustain me with a willing spirit.

Psalm 51:10–12

Oh, to be clinging once more! David had tasted the fruit of sin—not the aspect of fleeting pleasure but of feeling far from God. He wanted a clean heart, to be washed "whiter than snow" (Psalm 51:7), so He could be near to God again.

As believers, we have Jesus's promise, "I am with you always, even to the end of the age" (Matthew 28:20). We do not have to fear being ushered from the presence of God as Adam and Eve were, or of losing the Spirit of God. Nevertheless, sin has an impact on our relationship with God.

Please know that I'm not talking about the everyday ways in which we fall short. With the daily battle between flesh and Spirit, I might fall short several times in a single day—such as when I give my husband an eye roll, even if it's only in the corner of my heart. Hopefully, though, we are capturing those moments and clinging to God as we ask forgiveness.

But some sins persist. It doesn't have to be a "big sin" such as immorality—though, sadly, many of us are familiar with modern-day stories like David's, where a pastor, a fellow church member, or a friend who was once on fire for God falls into an extramarital affair. Our problem might be holding a grudge against another person, refusing to forgive. It might be getting caught up in selfish ambition. It may even be neglecting time in the Word, which is itself disobedience to the Word.

Wherever sin festers, that's an area of the heart that is not clinging to God. And "a little leaven leavens the whole lump of dough" (Galatians 5:9). It's a wedge that hinders us from dwelling as closely to God as we otherwise could. The Bible tells us, "Do not be deceived, God is not mocked; for whatever a man sows, this he will also reap. For the one who sows to his own flesh will from the flesh reap corruption, but the one who sows to the Spirit will from the Spirit reap eternal life" (Galatians 6:7–8).

On the positive side, this is an amazing promise: if we are sowing time with God, including prayer and study of the Word, we will reap intimacy with God. It's a spiritual truth. On the other hand, if we are sowing thoughts, motives, and behaviors contrary to the will of God, we reap "corruption." That's such an interesting word—it was used in the Greek to indicate decay, a wasting away. In other words, it's a downward slope. In this case, our intimacy with God suffers ruin.

Why is this the case? Because we cannot please God in the flesh (Romans 8:8), which is why we are called to die to the flesh. The flesh is directly opposed to the Spirit (Galatians 5:17), and it fights for dominance. When we cater to it, the flesh grows stronger while the influence of the Spirit in our lives weakens.

For example, if that eye roll in the corner of my heart toward my husband goes unchecked, it could become a habit—because my flesh is encouraged. I might begin to openly roll my eyes, raise my voice an octave or two, disregard his ideas and opinions because I consider my own as better. All the while, I'm in sin—because God has called me to respect and submit to my husband. And all the while, that attitude is a wedge, putting distance not only between Bill and me, but between myself and God, because I'm outside His will.

Thankfully, this is not about being perfect, or else we'd lose hope. Thankfully, too, God loves us unconditionally. We are forever and gloriously His, and for eternity we will enjoy His presence. But, here and now, we can enjoy the fullness of His presence. We can experience the full blessing of abundant life in Christ. By His grace, as we daily grow in obedience, we can die to our flesh and allow the Spirit to take control of our lives. In doing so, we are planting seeds, seeds that will produce a thriving relationship with the Lord.

Jesus Is Our Perfect Example

Jesus is the only person who has walked this earth free from sin, and He is the only one who dwelled in perfect intimacy with the Father.

Yes, He was God in flesh—but we cannot discount the fact that He *put on* flesh. He understands the battle between flesh and Spirit. "We do not have a high priest who cannot sympathize with our weaknesses, but One who has been tempted in all things as we are, yet without sin" (Hebrews 4:15). In Jesus's life we see the importance not only of obedience, but of turning quickly from temptation when it arises. And temptation reared its head early in His ministry.

Isn't it interesting that Satan, who targeted Eve and Job and David (and many others) would also target Jesus? He knew who Jesus was, of course. All the demons did. He knew Jesus was in the beginning with God, that He *was* God, and that all things were created by Him—including those angelic beings that were cast from heaven.

Still, Satan targeted *Jesus*, which tells me that no one is immune from temptation. If Jesus could be tempted, any of us can. I think that's comforting to know. It's also comforting to keep in mind that temptation does not equal sin—it's just an enticement toward sin. The enemy's goal, always, is to drive a wedge between us and God.

As with Eve, the Bible gives a firsthand look at the enemy's words as he came to tempt Jesus. Satan arrived after Jesus had fasted forty days and forty nights. In the enemy's mind, this was an opportune time—Jesus had to be weak from hunger.

Jesus had been baptized just prior to the fast—the Holy Spirit, as a dove, had alighted on Jesus, and the Father's voice had boomed from heaven, "This is My beloved Son, in whom I am well-pleased" (Matthew 3:17). The divine Trinity had shone itself publicly as One. The enemy couldn't have that—he would drive a wedge into the intimacy within the Godhead itself.

Satan opened with a challenge. "If You are the Son of God, command that these stones become bread" (Matthew 4:3).

"If You are the Son of God . . ."

Just as he'd done with Eve, the enemy took God's words and twisted them to his advantage. Implicit in the challenge was that God had been holding out on Jesus—the same message Satan had used with Eve.

She was being denied choice fruit; Jesus was being denied sustenance in the wilderness. But He was the Son of God, right? He could snap His fingers and feast!

It's funny—not long after, Jesus would feed more than five thousand people from a meager five loaves and two fish, with twelve basketsful left over. But that would be to fulfill the Father's purpose, not His own. "My food is to do the will of Him who sent Me and to accomplish His work" (John 4:34), Jesus would later say.

He didn't need to prove who He was with a fancy show of signs and wonders. That would've been motivated by pride, and Jesus had come in humility. Further, He didn't need to provide for Himself—He trusted the Father, who would send angels to minister to Jesus once the enemy departed.

So Jesus replied to Satan, "It is written, 'Man shall not live on bread alone, but on every word that proceeds out of the mouth of God'" (Matthew 4:4).

Unlike Eve, who was a little shaky as to what God had said, Jesus knew exactly. He refused to act against the will of God, which would have put a rift in His oneness with the Father. He made clear that clinging to God—through obedience and clinging to His Word—is more important than any earthly desire we may have.

Jesus had quoted Scripture in response to the first temptation, so the enemy took his turn at it. With his second temptation, Satan quoted one of my favorite psalms, the ninety-first, and in particular, this portion:

"For it is written, 'He will command His angels concerning You'; and
'On their hands they will bear You up,
So that You will not strike Your foot against a stone.'"

Matthew 4:6 (see Psalm 91:11–12)

I love the protection that Psalm 91 describes, the promise that we are under the charge of angels who guard us in all our ways. A year ago, Quentin was driving in a downpour, and the SUV hit a slick spot and ran into a light pole on the sidewalk. The pole fell on top of the car, crushing the roof and shattering the windows—on the passenger side. Quentin emerged with only a scratch. He said Psalm 91 came to mind, because he knew he'd experienced God's protection.

But in invoking Psalm 91, the enemy wasn't looking to illumine God's goodness and protection. Once again, he sought to move Jesus outside the will of God. As they stood atop the pinnacle of the temple, Satan said, "If You are the Son of God, throw Yourself down; for it is written, 'He will command His angels concerning You'" (Matthew 4:6).

It's one thing to see God's protection in the midst of calamity. It's quite another to *create* the calamity and expect God to show up. And we don't have to act as brazenly as throwing ourselves from a pinnacle. In pursuing our own plans and schemes, we can put ourselves in unwise positions because we didn't consult the Lord—and yet expect the Lord to run to our rescue. We can even put ourselves in the way of temptation, then cry out for help when it takes us farther than we wanted to go.

Jesus knew that wasn't the truth of Psalm 91, and we too have to know the whole counsel of the Word. He replied, "On the other hand, it is written, 'You shall not put the Lord Your God to the test'" (Matthew 4:7). Jesus didn't need to test God's faithfulness to His Word, and He certainly wouldn't go against the Word itself. In our own lives, God is often gracious to rescue us even when we've put ourselves in dubious positions. But the ultimate place of blessing and protection, always, is in His will.

The enemy revealed his true intent with the third temptation. On a high mountain, Satan showed Jesus the kingdoms of the world, saying, "All these things I will give You, if You fall down and worship me" (Matthew 4:9). He wanted Jesus to forsake the Most High God and worship the enemy of God. Declare Satan worthy of praise. Give him honor and glory.

Picture it—Jesus entering into an alliance with the god of this world! The unity of Father and Son would be shattered, their intimacy no more. And if there's no intimacy between Father and Son, there's no intimacy with God for the rest of us. The entire redemptive plan for the world would be ruined.

The enemy's offer sounds ludicrous to us. No way would the King of Kings and Lord of Lords be swayed by such a temptation—He will one day rule the nations in power and glory. But would the offer sound as ludicrous with respect to you and me? What if Satan offered *you* the kingdoms of the world and their glory?

Oh, the enemy would be more subtle, of course, and tailor it to Christian sensibilities. Maybe he holds out a platform to showcase your gifts and talents, with book deals, speaking engagements, and thousands of followers around the world. But it's understood that you're to be a "motivational" speaker only. Encourage people to be all they can be, to pursue purpose and calling. But tell them, "the power is in you" or "the universe." If you speak of God, keep it general. "Jesus" offends.

Believers are not immune to such temptations. And whenever we move toward the love of the world and the things of the world, we move away from our God. "For all that is in the world, the lust of the flesh and the lust of the eyes and the boastful pride of life, is not from the Father, but is from the world" (1 John 2:16)—and the world is under the control of the evil one. Bowing to the dictates of the world is akin to bowing to the enemy. It's a sobering truth, but one we do well to bear in mind so that we are not deceived. Jesus replied: "Go, Satan! For it is written, 'You shall worship the LORD your God, and serve Him only'" (Matthew 4:10).

Only.

Clinging to God means devotion to God is our highest priority. In choosing a lifestyle of intimacy with Him, we choose a lifestyle of walking by the Spirit, of doing the things that please God, by His grace. But we know the enemy is not pleased with that heart posture. We *will* be tempted, in one way or another. And it will come at an opportune time and appeal to us personally—making it harder to resist. But the Spirit gives us power to resist, and will bring to mind Scripture that exposes the temptation for what it is. Like Jesus, we resist by clinging to truth, which is yet another reason to grow in our knowledge of the truth.

When it comes to temptation, Jesus also gives us these pointed words: "Keep watching and praying that you may not enter into temptation; the spirit is willing, but the flesh is weak" (Matthew 26:41). Because of the weakness of our flesh, we *have* to cling to God continually, ever looking to Him, ever prayerful. We don't know what schemes the enemy will devise, and we don't have to know. We simply keep our eyes fixed on the Lord, who supplies lavish grace and strength to avoid the pitfalls. And we praise Him that if we do fall, like David did, God supplies lavish grace, strength, and forgiveness for us to get back up and hold fast to Him once more.

Intimacy and obedience are tied. If I'm entangled in sin, I'm not clinging. I'm not manifesting my love for the Lord, who said, "If you love Me, you will keep My commandments" (John 14:15). But when, despite our flesh and momentary failings, we hold fast to God, we are growing in "the love of Christ which surpasses knowledge" (Ephesians 3:19). Our intimacy with Him is increased. And we enjoy the immeasurable blessing of being "filled up to all the fullness of God" (Ephesians 3:19).

8

Healing from
Immoral Clinging

Everyone in the city knew who she was, and not for her admirable deeds. She wasn't like Martha, known for hospitality and serving, even if she sometimes overdid it (see Luke 10:38–42). She wasn't like Tabitha, so known for kindness and charity that widows wept when she died, before God used Peter to raise her back to life (see Acts 9:36–41). And she certainly wasn't like Mary, a virgin till her wedding day, known in the heavenly realm as highly favored.

No, this woman isn't even given a name. She is known only by that which defined her—sin. That's what marked her life. She was the kind of woman—the "strange woman"—whom the father in Proverbs warns against:

For her house sinks down to death
And her tracks lead to the dead;
None who go to her return again,
Nor do they reach the paths of life.

Proverbs 2:18–19

One of the father's goals in sharing his wisdom was to keep his son from such a woman (Proverbs 6:23–24). Unlike the excellent wife who does her man good all the days of her life, the immoral woman brings harm like taking fire to one's bosom or walking on hot coals (6:27–28). So the father warns again:

> *Now then, my sons, listen to me*
> *And do not depart from the words of my mouth.*
> *Keep your way far from her*
> *And do not go near the door of her house.*

Proverbs 5:7–8

Keep your way far from her.

This was how people felt about the woman, the "sinner," who encountered Jesus. She was likely a prostitute. And though there were men who happily exploited her, none respected her. In polite society, they shunned her for the immoral woman she was. And she knew. She knew her place.

Until something compelled her to move beyond convention, beyond the inevitable ridicule, beyond *herself.* She heard that Jesus was in her city, reclining at the home of Simon the Pharisee, and she had to see Him.[1]

She must have felt a great deal of trepidation. Many would be there curious to see and hear Jesus up close, and the door would be open to receive them. But she herself wouldn't be welcome. If given the chance, the Pharisees would have stoned her. So what would Simon say to her? Would she be turned away?

Actually, she didn't know what Jesus would do or say either. But wasn't He also ridiculed, as the friend of sinners? She couldn't have been sure of much—except that she had to go see Jesus. But first, she grabbed her precious alabaster vial of perfume.

At Simon's house, the woman slipped in among those who were gathered. The room was likely dimly lit, so she could lurk in the

---

1. The following is an interpretation of the scene depicted in Luke 7:36–50. The quotes are taken verbatim from the passage.

background unnoticed. Carefully, she surveyed the men reclining at the low dining table. If Simon were to spot her, she might be put out. And there was the one she sought—*Jesus*. She moved closer. She had to. And as she got closer, she was overcome. Standing behind Him now at His feet, tears poured from her eyes—from the depths of her heart. She could see her life. The men. The things she'd done with her body. She felt filthy. And ashamed. She couldn't stop weeping.

People were starting to stare, but she didn't care. She lowered herself, and her tears wet His feet. Why were His feet dirty? Simon hadn't made sure his guest's feet were washed? Then she would wash them herself.

She let down her hair. People would frown on that too. It just wasn't done. But this was how she would clean and dry Jesus's feet. This was how she would worship Him.

Worship. It surprised even her, yet that's what was in her heart. Worshipping Jesus. No matter what some said about Him, this man was Lord and Savior. She just *knew* it.

Jesus didn't seem put off as the woman wiped His feet with her hair. He didn't move them aside. He didn't stiffen uncomfortably. *Strange*, she thought. As unworthy as she felt in His presence, she also felt welcomed by Him. *He* would welcome *her*? Would allow her to touch Him? Didn't He know who she was and what she'd done?

Her heart overflowed with gratitude and love. Without thinking, swept away by His goodness toward her, she began kissing His feet, tears ever falling. Then she opened her alabaster vial of perfume. It was costly, but even that brought more shame, considering how she'd earned the money. But this seemed fitting—to anoint Jesus.

Still kissing His feet, she poured the perfume on them, realizing this action would bring great attention to herself, if she hadn't already. The room filled with the scent. Heads were turning, among them, Simon's. The look in his eyes made her shrink inside. Maybe she'd gone too far. Maybe this was all wrong . . .

"Simon, I have something to say to you," Jesus said suddenly.

The woman, poised at His feet, listened as her tears fell silently. Simon replied, "Say it, Teacher."

Jesus, reclining still, said, "A moneylender had two debtors: one owed five hundred denarii, and the other fifty. When they were unable to repay, he graciously forgave them both. So which of them will love him more?"

The faces around the room seemed to reflect the woman's own thoughts. What was this about?

"I suppose the one whom he forgave more," Simon said.

Jesus said, "You have judged correctly."

Then He shifted and turned toward her, and said, "Do you see this woman?"

Her heart raced. *Me?*

Jesus continued, "I entered your house; you gave Me no water for My feet, but she has wet My feet with her tears and wiped them with her hair. You gave Me no kiss; but she, since the time I came in, has not ceased to kiss My feet. You did not anoint My head with oil, but she anointed My feet with perfume."

Eyes lowered, she continued to embrace His feet, overwhelmed. He was talking, with admiration, about something she did?

"For this reason I say to you," Jesus said, "her sins, which are many, have been forgiven, for she loved much; but he who is forgiven little, loves little."

Her sins, which are many . . . So He knew. He really did know who she was and what she'd done. And of course—He was the Messiah. Still, to hear Him say it out loud, in front of everyone . . .

But wait, what was the rest? Did He say her sins had been *forgiven*?

Jesus turned his gaze from Simon to the woman. Her breath caught.

"Your sins have been forgiven," Jesus said.

He said it again. With no qualifiers. No preconditions. It was *done*. She'd been forgiven.

The room was quiet, as if others were marveling like she was at the gift He'd given her. She could hardly process it. *Forgiven?* An indescribable weight had been lifted. She was free. Everything in her wanted to twirl around the room.

Jesus was still looking at her. "Your faith has saved you; go in peace."

Do You Struggle with an Immoral Past?

We might think we can't identify with this particular woman because she was a prostitute. For many of us, if we've even seen a prostitute, she was on television or the big screen, steeped in stereotype. "The world's oldest profession" is a world far from ours—and we might regard her story as unrelatable.

But when we get to the heart of it, is it truly foreign? How many of us can say we've escaped the taint of sexual immorality? Or maybe I should ask how many of us have even *tried* to escape it? In the world, sex is a natural part of a relationship between consenting adults, and often, teens. To abstain, to deny physical and emotional desires until marriage—that's what's odd. People say it's okay to abstain for a limited time, until the relationship reaches a certain stage or one finds "the right guy." But at some point, sex is in view.

That was my mind-set. My mother had preached abstinence until marriage, but it was founded on her opinion—because that's what she'd done. Though my mom is a strong believer now, she didn't know the Lord when she was rearing me. Still, the grace of God was at work in her life, especially in wisdom like this that she tried to impart. But I dismissed it as old-fashioned morals. Instead, I constructed my own, with ideals as to who the right guy would be and what the wait time should be. And in all the packaging of what would be "special" and "proper" and "respectable," there was one truth—sex was in view. In time, like the woman with the alabaster vial of perfume, I came to Jesus with the stain of becoming "one flesh" outside of marriage.

Even if it's a one-time only experience, sex is affecting. It reaches to the depths of the soul, as it was designed to do. In Genesis, after Eve was presented to Adam as his wife, God gave this timeless truth:

*"For this reason a man shall leave his father and his mother, and be joined
to his wife; and they shall become one flesh."*

Genesis 2:24

"Be joined" is also translated "cleave" or "hold fast," all of which
originate from that same Hebrew word (*dabaq*) that's also rendered
cling. God designed marriage in such a way that a husband and wife
would *cling* to one another and become *one flesh*. Jesus, during His
earthly ministry, repeated this Genesis verse, adding, "So they are no
longer two, but one flesh" (Matthew 19:5–6).

But while husband and wife become one flesh in marriage, because
of the way God designed our bodies, sex *outside* of marriage also causes
a man and woman to become one flesh. In both cases, becoming "one
flesh" has spiritual implications: for husband and wife, it is sanctifying
and holy; for two who aren't married, it is corrupting. In fact, the "one
flesh" nature of sex makes it a sin unlike any other. The apostle Paul
put it this way: "Every other sin that a man commits is outside the
body, but the immoral man sins against his own body" (1 Corinthians
6:18). In explaining why this is so, he references Genesis 2:24: "For
He says, 'The two shall become one flesh.'"

Do you see how this also relates to clinging? In marriage, clinging and
becoming one flesh go hand in hand. In the same way, as we become
one flesh with another person outside the covenant of marriage, our
souls invariably cling, in one way or another. It is natural to be emo-
tionally tied to that man, to feel bonded, to want commitment—and
to be heartbroken when things don't work out.

Even if it's understood that the sex is "casual," you can't force your soul
to believe it. What's spiritual can never be casual. Whether one realizes it
or not, the soul is holding fast—to a person, to a longing to be loved, to
a desire to feel worthy, to a lie that you're unworthy, to the lie that you
can enjoy the pleasures of sexual sin without the spiritual consequences.

The bottom line in all of this is a clinging far different than we've
been discussing. It's a *counterfeit clinging*, an *immoral clinging*. Rather
than holding fast to God, our place of blessing and protection, this

is a holding fast to that which damages to the core—even if we don't realize it.

But by the grace of God, He allows us to feel the emptiness of that path. The brokenness. The pain. The loneliness. The shame. These are the things that drive us to Jesus, like the woman with the alabaster vial. And yet, even with forgiveness, many struggle with the emotional and spiritual fallout from their sexual past.

Is that you? Do you struggle from time to time with your past? I ask this understanding that for one person, the past may be twenty or thirty years ago, and for another, two or three months ago. It may also be that your struggle has to do with unwanted sexual behavior forced upon you. The pain is tremendous, the effects far-reaching. Do you feel unworthy to choose a lifestyle of intimacy with God because of the intimacy you've shared with others?

My prayer is that the Lord will use this chapter to help you stand firm in the forgiveness, freedom, and healing you've been given in Christ. I talked about the inherent nature of sex and the soul's desire to cling not as an exercise in pop psychology, but because we need to understand spiritual truths revealed in the Word of God. This nature of sex gives us insight as to why we may struggle—because our souls were deeply affected.

But our main focus has to be Jesus, without whom we could never be healed. In Him, our healing is complete. I *so* want you to grab hold of "the breadth and length and height and depth" (Ephesians 3:18) of Jesus's unconditional love for you. For *you*. He wants you to be healed completely. The grace of God is more powerful than your past.

So let's go back to Simon's house to make sure we glean the truths that bring healing to our souls.

But first . . .

Don't Miss the Aerial View

When we look at accounts of Jesus's life, such as this story of a woman with an alabaster vial, we focus on what occurred on that particular occasion, as we should. But it's encouraging also to step back and get a big-picture view.

The Gospels cover only a portion of Jesus's earthly ministry. Far more occurred than what was written. John, author of the fourth Gospel, says, "Therefore many other signs Jesus also performed in the presence of the disciples, which are not written in this book; but these have been written so that you may believe that Jesus is the Christ, the Son of God; and that believing you may have life in His name" (John 20:30–31).

Thus, there is purpose in what is included—that we would believe and have life in His name. Also, there is intentionality in what is included, since "all Scripture is inspired by God" (2 Timothy 3:16). In a very real sense, the specific events that we know about Jesus's life have been hand-picked by God. How striking, then, that significant space is devoted to encounters that Jesus had with *immoral* women, not perfect ones.

This alone is a tremendous comfort and encouragement. What if we only saw Jesus interact with women like His mother, Mary, or the admirable Mary who sat at His feet to learn from Him? What if they were all holy and near-perfect? If we didn't become immediately discouraged, we would strive for perfection ourselves . . . and *then* become discouraged.

Instead, we see women who are flawed and stained. We see ourselves. And our gaze can't help but move to Jesus, who receives them—and us—with lavish love and grace.

Our God wanted us to *know* this. He wanted His Word to include these stories about real women with real issues who were forever changed by a living God. He wanted us to know that He doesn't expect us to be perfect.

He wanted us to know that He doesn't view us through the lens of our past.

So we're able to behold incredible encounters like the one between Jesus and the woman at the well, which we'll feast on below. And of course, we have this incredible story of the woman with the alabaster vial of perfume. In this one encounter, there is so much to glean and rejoice in.

From Shame to Glory Story

We may be tempted to think that our sexual past brings Jesus shame, perhaps because we ourselves feel shame. Or we're afraid to admit we even have a past, and thus are slow to share our testimony for fear of somehow being less of a Christian. *What would people think if they knew?*

But Jesus showed us quite the opposite in Simon's home. Though everyone knew the facts about this woman who kissed and anointed His feet, He didn't distance Himself from her. He showed no discomfort or embarrassment. He didn't indicate in the least that He'd rather not associate with her.

Moreover, Jesus didn't downplay her display. He could have—He might have let her worship silently and quietly slip out, without His saying a word. People simply would have been left to speculate how He felt about her. They might have assumed that He didn't know who the woman was, which is what Simon assumed: "Now when the Pharisee who had invited Him saw this, he said to himself, 'If this man were a prophet He would know who and what sort of person this woman is who is touching Him, that she is a sinner'" (Luke 7:39).

But look at the next verse: "And Jesus answered him, 'Simon, I have something to say to you.'" Don't you love that? Simon was *thinking* these things, yet Jesus heard. As sovereign God, He knew what Simon and everyone else in the room was thinking. He knew they were waiting to see what He would do about this awkward display with a "sinner." But rather than downplay the situation, Jesus brought it out into the open.

There was no shame in it. The room saw a sinner. Jesus saw a woman filled with sorrow over the life she'd lived. He saw a woman being transformed. Far from shame, it was a glory story. Jesus would lift her from the shadows and bring her center stage. He would, in effect, tell everyone to take note, as her past became a glorious object lesson.

Let's look again at that parable Jesus told, and think about our own lives:

"A moneylender had two debtors: one owed five hundred denarii, and the other fifty. When they were unable to repay, he graciously forgave them both. So which of them will love him more?"

Luke 7:41–42

When we think about the sin debt we owed, we know we could have never paid it short of eternal death. Being graciously forgiven is a gift for which we are forever grateful. Yet Jesus added a twist. In Christ, we're all forgiven, but our worship may be different. The one who owed more—the "bigger sinner," so to speak—will know deeper worship.

Have you considered that? The very thing in your past that causes you grief is the very thing that propels your worship. You *know* how far you were from the Lord. You know what it was like to be in the pit of darkness. And you're astounded that the Lord would choose you and deliver you from darkness into the marvelous light. Your heart overflows with gratitude. Your love deepens when you think of it. *That's* how you should think about your past—as a springboard for your worship. It makes me want to praise right now!

But first, we have to look again at the way Jesus exalted this woman in front of everyone:

Turning toward the woman, He said to Simon, "Do you see this woman? I entered your house; you gave Me no water for My feet, but she has wet My feet with her tears and wiped them with her hair. You gave Me no kiss; but she, since the time I came in, has not ceased to kiss My feet. You did not anoint My head with oil, but she anointed My feet with perfume. For this reason I say to you, her sins, which are many, have been forgiven, for she loved much; but he who is forgiven little, loves little."

Luke 7:44–47

This was a woman whose life bore this description from the Proverbs: "Her feet go down to death, her steps take hold of Sheol. She does not ponder the path of life; her ways are unstable, she does not know it" (Proverbs 5:5–6). But it's not the same woman now. She's a woman who met Jesus, and that makes *all* the difference. Her steps were going down to death, but Jesus turned them toward life. And now, Jesus was heaping grace, favor, and honor upon her. That is gloriously astounding.

Please, if you struggle with your past, embrace this truth for yourself. Believe that you are not the same woman. In Christ, you are a new creation: "the old things passed away; behold, new things have come" (2 Corinthians 5:17). Some will focus on those old things in your life— but as for you, focus on the new things. Behold them . . . continually! Through Jesus you have been blessed abundantly, more than you or I can even fathom. And the "new" is happening constantly as we change little by little into the image of Christ. Believe that *He* sees you new, in Him. Believe that you too have a glory story, because you do.

Your past holds no shame. Only the enemy would seek to accuse you for something that's been covered by the blood of Jesus. And if Satan does accuse you—if you find your thoughts filling anew with shame—remember your springboard. Turn it to praise! Yes, that's who you used to be—*but God!* Meditate on the truth Jesus shared in Simon's home. Let your past deepen your worship and adoration of the Savior, as you praise Him for setting you free.

And don't forget this glorious truth: it was Jesus who first knew you and loved you, before time began—just as He knew the woman with the alabaster vial of perfume. He knew the life she would lead. And when Simon invited Him to dinner, Jesus knew she would be there. That moment had been appointed. Jesus knew she would one day be His.

Each of our lives is special in that way. We can stand on the truth that Jesus knew everything we would do—the worst of the worst— and He loved us and chose us anyway. In His time, He made Himself known to us. *He pursued us.* We see this beautifully in His encounter with the woman at the well.

Another Immoral Woman . . . More Lavish Grace

She was unlike the woman at the home of Simon the Pharisee. She hadn't come looking for Jesus. Her heart hadn't been moved to worship Him with kisses and tears and the sweet aroma of perfume. In her corner of the world, she didn't know who Jesus was. For her, it was an ordinary day consisting of everyday tasks like drawing water from the well.

But while she knew nothing about Jesus, Jesus knew all about her. And He came to her town—for her.[2]

He was walking with His disciples from Judea to Galilee, from the southern portion of Israel toward the north. Scripture says, "And He had to pass through Samaria" (John 4:4). That's a line we might skim past, as a kind of geographic footnote. But, from a physical standpoint, Jesus didn't *have* to pass through Samaria. Although Samaria was en route, Jewish people routinely bypassed it as they traveled. They didn't like the Samaritan people, who were considered half-breeds, descendants of Jewish people who'd intermingled with foreigners in the land after Assyria had conquered the Northern Kingdom of Israel centuries before.

But Jesus had a divine appointment with a Samaritan woman that day. He had to pass through.

Weary, Jesus sat by a well while His disciples went to buy food. It was about noon when the woman came to draw water. The scene was set, with just the two of them. And the scene itself amazes me.

Let's return to that aerial view for a moment. We rarely read of a private encounter between Jesus and just one other person. Nicodemus comes to mind, the Jewish ruler who visited Jesus at night. But though we might assume they were alone, the text doesn't actually say so. There could have been a disciple or two listening.

Typically, we read of Jesus speaking to a crowd, or at least to His disciples. If He's in a home, He's often with others—as at Simon's

---

2. This account of Jesus and the woman at the well is taken from John 4. Specific verse citations are omitted for the sake of the flow of the dialogue.

house or the home of Mary and Martha. Once, when He was home in Capernaum, it was so crowded that men had to let down a paralytic through the roof (Mark 2:1–4). If Jesus wanted to be alone to pray, He had to slip away to a secluded place.

But remarkably, Jesus in John 4 met one-on-one with someone. Even more remarkably, it was a woman. Customarily, this wasn't done, especially by rabbis. In fact, when His disciples later returned, they "were amazed" that He'd been speaking with a woman (John 4:27). But Jesus wasn't bound by social and cultural norms. It didn't matter that this person was a Samaritan or a woman or even—as we learn—an immoral woman.

If His disciples had been present, the dynamic would have been different. She may have been reticent to engage Him. Whatever the case, Jesus knew. And He was willing to meet her where she was, privately, in order to minister to her as only He could.

The setting of this scene alone should encourage us. Jesus is this intentional with each of us. He knows how to draw us. He chooses the setting and the timing. He knows the people He will use, or if necessary, dismiss. He meets us exactly where we are.

The Samaritan woman came to the well, and she proceeded to draw water. Maybe she saw Jesus, but I wouldn't be surprised if she averted her gaze. She would take care of her business and leave.

It was Jesus who started the dialogue. Oh, how I love that simple fact. "Give me a drink," He said.

She was surely startled. Jesus knows how to capture our attention, doesn't He? Maybe she looked at Jesus a little funny as she said, "How is it that You, being a Jew, ask me for a drink since I am a Samaritan woman?"

Jewish people didn't like her people. Plus, He was a man. Everything was wrong with this picture. *What is His deal?* she must have thought.

This woman saw the earthly distinctions between them. Jesus saw the spiritual. It wasn't about Samaritan and Jewish or male and female;

it was about sinner and Savior. She needed to see herself and Him with new eyes. Jesus began to elevate her sight.

Jesus said, "If you knew the gift of God, and who it is who says to you, 'Give me a drink,' you would have asked Him, and He would have given you living water."

Though He had just met her, He knew this woman. He knew her sordid story. And immediately, He offered her a gift *from God*. When we've been living a life that's not pleasing to God, the last thing we expect is that He'd come bearing gifts. Judgment maybe, but not a gift. And all she had to do was ask?

The Samaritan woman replied, "Sir, You have nothing to draw with and the well is deep; where then do You get that living water? You are not greater than our Father Jacob, are You, who gave us the well, and drank of it himself and his sons and his cattle?"

You have to give it to her. She'd been around the block, and she had questions. And maybe it's my own bent, but I kind of hear a smart-alecky tone. I totally get it! A free gift from God of "living water"? Yeah, right. Is this guy even for real?

Jesus, ever patient, once again moved to lift this woman's perspective from the earthly to the spiritual. "Everyone who drinks of this water will thirst again; but whoever drinks of the water that **I will give him** shall never thirst; but the water that **I will give him** will become in him a well of water springing up to eternal life."

I bolded "I will give him" because Jesus gave it emphasis. He was letting the woman know that *He* is the giver of this water, which has nothing to do with a well or an implement to draw from the well. Moreover, this was water she'd never tasted. In fact, this water was so special that when she drank it, she would never thirst again—and she'd have a well *inside* her, an eternal, life-giving well.

Huh? Never thirst again? Can't you see her pondering Jesus's words? Who could deny an offer like that? It sounded too good to be true. But, hey—might as well go for it. "Sir, give me this water, so I will not be thirsty nor come all the way here to draw."

This was where she'd see if He was for real. Didn't He say to ask? Well, she asked. She would see what this "living water" was all about and whether He could deliver.

And then this:

"Go, call your husband and come here."

The woman had to have been thrown. *Call my husband? What in the world does that have to do with water?* And knowing her own situation, she must have stammered when she said, "I have no husband."

Jesus said, "You have correctly said, 'I have no husband'; for you have had five husbands, and the one whom you now have is not your husband; this you have said truly."

And just like that, He read this woman her past. Suddenly she stood naked before Him. But don't you read a calmness in Jesus's voice? No accusation or judgment. He's stating facts, even acknowledging her honesty. Yet, those facts are convicting. She needed to hear them to finally understand that this was no ordinary Jewish man—her next words were, "Sir, I perceive that You are a prophet." She also needed to come face-to-face with her sin. That's the only way she could grasp the free gift of the living water.

I imagine the Samaritan woman's head was spinning about now. *Who is this man? What do I even say, given that He sees right through me?* One thing was sure—she was no longer talking about earthly things. Now she asked about proper places of worship. Jesus shared with her the beautiful truth that, "God is spirit, and those who worship Him must worship in spirit and truth," after which there was surely a pause . . .

This is what we know. The Holy Spirit had been drawing this woman through that entire conversation. Slowly, her eyes were being opened to who this Man was—even as He exposed who she was. Like the woman with the alabaster vial of perfume, she likely felt the shame of what she'd done, yet also the loving welcome of Jesus's presence. Words He'd uttered undoubtedly ran back through her mind. Gift of God . . . living water . . . eternal life.

She said to Jesus, "I know that Messiah is coming (He who is called Christ); when that One comes, He will declare all things to us."

She knew about the promised Messiah. Her heart was on edge. It couldn't be, not right here before her . . .

The words that follow make my heart soar every time.

"Jesus said to her, 'I who speak to you am He.'"

Whoa! Why does my heart soar? Because Jesus rarely told people plainly that He was the Messiah. Yet He told this woman—a woman living in an immoral relationship even as they spoke, but who would come away changed. He passed through Samaria for this one woman, to free her from sin, from thirsting for what would never satisfy, from steps that lead down to death . . . to give her *life*.

This is the same Jesus who rescued you and me. He saw us thirsting and trying to fill our thirsts ourselves. He saw us clinging to people and ways that fractured our souls. He said, **I will give you** living water so that you never have to thirst again, so that you never have to cling to counterfeits again. He gave us *life*.

And like the Samaritan woman, we needn't be ashamed of who we used to be. She went into the city immediately, telling people to come see this Man who told her all the things she'd done. Clearly, they knew what she'd done as well. She didn't care. It was a testimony now, and she was going to tell it. They came to Jesus in droves, and many more believed. God *used* her to lead others to Christ on the basis of her past.

How powerful is that? It's no wonder the enemy seeks to shame and silence us when it comes to our past. He knows how powerful a testimony it is. He knows how deep the worship is. He knows how many others would be moved by the love, grace, and forgiveness we received in Christ. The enemy would much rather remind us of our old deeds than of the forgiveness we received.

But that forgiveness was bought by the blood of Jesus. We can never forget the debt we owed, and the price He paid. Because of Him, our transgressions are cast far from us, as far as the east is from the west (Psalm 103:12). "Therefore there is now no condemnation for those who are in Christ Jesus" (Romans 8:1). The shame was buried with those old thirsts. We are now vessels of grace, daughters of the Most High God who will live eternally with Him.

I can't wait to meet the woman with the alabaster vial of perfume and the Samaritan woman, sisters whose sins were many, and whose love for the Savior runs deep as a result.

My dear sister, walk in the newness of life Jesus has given. Grow in His grace. Love and worship Him to your core. And allow Him to use you to tell others about our Lord, who seeks, saves, and lavishly loves women like you and me.

9

Clinging to Hopes, Dreams, and Callings

I still remember the inner tug-of-war I felt as I contemplated walking away from my career. The idea had been building in my heart for a while. I'd even reduced my hours, at least on paper, a year and a half before. But that was the problem—in civil litigation, it was next to impossible to work reduced hours. When a client needed me, I had to be there. When there were briefs due, motions to file, depositions to conduct, arguments to be made before the court, and colleagues who counted on my work . . . I had to be there.

Yet I found myself wanting to be home. That was new for me. I'd been taught to be financially independent. I dreamed of having a successful career, and when I decided on law, I envisioned a partnership at a high-powered firm and, maybe later, a judgeship. I was on my way. I had worked up through the associate ranks at my firm—a large Milwaukee-based law firm—and had been voted into partnership the year before. I was making a six-figure salary, Bill and I had bought a beautiful new home, and I could see the pathway to continued success. But the Lord was working something different in my heart.

It was undeniable. Increasingly I had thoughts of spending my days with my kids, ages one and three, catching their "firsts," being their primary influence. The latter had to be fruit from a seed planted when I was pregnant with Quentin. On a trip to Southern California, Bill and I were at a restaurant for dinner, and our server—a delightful man from Germany—noticed I was expecting. "Be your child's primary influence," he said. "Make sure he smiles like you."

It was one of those moments that struck us as both odd and God-ordained. We never forgot the man's words. They were still in our minds as Bill and I talked about whether I would resign. On a road trip home from out east, driving through the mountains of West Virginia, we recounted all the ways the Lord had moved in our hearts to consider this change—including our German waiter. The more we talked, the clearer it became. This was what the Lord wanted us to do. And by this point, it was what *I* wanted to do. Still, I could feel the pull to cling to what I had.

What would it mean to give up my career? I had worked hard to be promoted to partner, and had only held the position for one year. There was so much more ahead. I didn't love the billable hour requirement and the long hours, but I'd been carving out a niche in trademark litigation and enjoying it. And I enjoyed my salary—let's keep it real. I liked having flexible spending options and the ability to invest for the future.

While a part of me wanted to cling to that life, I knew I had to cling to God and His will for our family in that season. By His grace, He'd been moving in Bill's heart and mine. We were excited about what the change would mean for our family. By the end of the road trip, we'd decided to do it. We would step out in faith.

In the months after I resigned, though, my heart was tested. It seemed every time I turned around, someone was asking the proverbial question, "So, what do you do?" One day I responded as I often had, "I'm an attorney, but I'm not practicing right now."

Conviction descended immediately. It was as if the Holy Spirit tapped me on the shoulder and said, "You can go ahead and cut that out."

The message rang loud and clear in my heart. I was clinging to my identity as an attorney and the aura of success it conveyed. While I enjoyed being with my kids, the "stay-at-home mom" title was hard to embrace. Hardly anyone I knew was a stay-at-home mom, and some questioned my walking away from my career. I'd often hear, "You're going back, right? When they hit school age?"

It felt like I was doing something "less than" what I'd been doing formerly. So part of me had lingered behind rather than following the Lord into this new season. My heart was divided. Even if only by a thread, I was holding onto what I'd had.

I knew the Lord wanted me to let that go—and not only the thread. What if I *never* returned to the practice of law? Would I be willing to lay it down completely, if that's what God called me to do? Was I willing to lay down my dream of a lucrative career, of financial security, of wearing a professional title that engendered respect? Was I willing to grow to the point where I could say, like the apostle Paul, "whatever things were gain to me, those things I have counted as loss for the sake of Christ" (Philippians 3:7)?

I didn't know what the future held, but from where I stood in that moment, I knew I needed to follow the Lord fully. Jesus said, "If anyone serves Me, he must follow Me; and where I am, there My servant will be also" (John 12:26). It sounds so simple, but notice the progression: by following, we are where Jesus is. Put another way, if we want to be where Jesus is—if we want to abide in Him—we have to follow Him, with a whole heart. Following is a close cousin to clinging.

Called to Follow

Maybe you've been there too, that moment you sense God calling you to leave a job, an organization, or anything else that's been a significant part of your life. Did you find it hard? Did you feel that it had become part of your identity—and you weren't sure who you'd be without it? It makes sense, since we often refer to people by what they do: teacher, accountant, librarian. It's natural to cling to those things, and to see them as lasting a lifetime. But we never know if and when God might switch things up.

Four of Jesus's disciples were fishermen. The two sets of brothers— Simon Peter and Andrew, and James and John—were business partners who spent their lives on the water with their nets. But Jesus began to shake up their livelihood.

It started with Andrew. He'd been a disciple of John the Baptist, and one day he heard John say, "Behold the Lamb of God!" (John 1:36). That was Jesus, and Andrew followed and spent the day with Him. Based on what he'd seen and heard, he went to his brother Simon and said, "We have found the Messiah" (John 1:41). Simon also came to Jesus, who renamed him Peter. But though Andrew and Peter spent significant time with Jesus for a while thereafter (together with other disciples), they didn't begin following Him in earnest. They went back to their trade—fishing.

Then one day Jesus was teaching by their place of employment, the lake. The crowd was pressing around Him while Peter and Andrew were busy on the job, cleaning their nets. Jesus got into Peter's boat and asked him to move a ways out, gaining some space from the crowd so He could teach. When Jesus was done teaching, He told Peter to move out further, and to let down his net for a catch.

Peter said, "Master we worked hard all night and caught nothing, but I will do as You say and let down the nets" (Luke 5:5).

Suddenly, so many fish filled the nets that they began to break. James and John were in the next boat and moved in to help, but both boats became so loaded with fish that they almost sank. The men were all amazed, and Peter fell at Jesus's feet and said, "Go away from me Lord, for I am a sinful man!" (Luke 5:8).

Jesus told them not to fear, and that from then on they would be fishers of men. Just like that, Jesus changed their occupation, and radically changed their lives. They had seen Jesus's glory and majesty. They believed He was the Christ, the Son of God. So on their most successful day in business, with the biggest catch of their lives, "they left everything and followed Him" (Luke 5:11).

Knowing Jesus changes everything. In our hearts, we too see His majesty and His glory. We believe He is Lord and Savior, and that we'll spend an eternity with Him. Yet there's also a cost here on earth. We take up our cross and *follow*. Jesus says, "He who has found his life will lose it, and he who has lost his life for My sake will find it" (Matthew 10:39).

We will not all be called to leave our field of work or other chosen endeavors, but we are all called to be willing. We are called to follow wherever He leads, such that we can cling.

The tie between following and clinging is seen way back in Deuteronomy, when Moses gave this instruction:

*"You shall **follow** the LORD your God and fear Him; and you shall keep His commandments, listen to His voice, serve Him, and **cling** to Him."*

Deuteronomy 13:4

God emphasized to the nation of Israel the importance of following and clinging to Him, just as Jesus emphasized to His disciples the importance of following and abiding in Him. That's the nature of the life of a believer: it's not a casual or halfhearted kind of following. For much of His ministry on earth, crowds followed Jesus. Some were curious. Others wanted what He could do for them, such as healing or multiplying fishes and loaves. But when Jesus began to speak of what was required of them, most went away.

Wrapped up with the words *follow* and *cling* is sacrifice. Just as Jesus laid down His life for us, we lay down our lives for Him. We let go of earthly hopes, dreams, and plans in order to follow God's divine plan, one He purposed for us before time began. In so doing, we walk by faith, not knowing what that plan will entail. But if it's God's plan, it's the only plan that is for our good and His glory. It's the plan that will bear much eternal fruit.

Peter, Andrew, James, and John didn't know what would happen when they left everything and followed Jesus. They hardly understood His ministry at that point, where it would lead, and what part they would play. But today we don't know them as fisherman. We know them as apostles, because they followed with a whole heart. That's the power of God's transforming work in our hearts and lives.

The details differ from person to person, but there's always a cost. We will have to stop clinging to *something*, often several somethings, in order to follow God and cling to Him. And then we can watch as He does a work in and through our lives that we could not have imagined. God is faithful. Following Him and clinging to Him are the pathway of blessing, no matter what we're called to let go. Indeed, when a life is fully yielded to God, we see His glory unmistakably—and beautifully.

How Much Would You Give to Follow and Cling?

The four fishermen left everything when Jesus said, "Follow Me." As radical a change as it was, though, they didn't have to move to a foreign country. Jesus's ministry was there in Israel. And they had the benefit of being *with* Jesus in the flesh, day in and day out, listening to Him and learning from Him. When I think of that contrasted with Abraham's call, I'm even more inspired by his faith.

When God appeared to him, Abram (as he was originally called) lived in Mesopotamia, specifically "Ur of the Chaldeans" (Genesis 11:31), which is modern-day Iraq. There is no indication that he had ever heard of the true and living God. His people worshipped other gods, a pantheon of them, including a chief god called Marduk. Capital of the ancient Chaldean empire, Ur was known as one of the great cities of the ancient world.

So when God appeared to Abram and said, "Go forth from your country, and from your relatives, and from your father's house, to the land which I will show you" (Genesis 12:1), it's astounding that Abram listened and followed! The four fishermen could look to the

Scriptures, which promised the Messiah's coming. And they'd heard Jesus's wisdom and seen His miracles before leaving life as they knew it. Abram, as God's chosen, had nothing but faith:

> *By faith, Abraham, when he was called, obeyed by going out to a place which he was to receive for an inheritance; and he went out, not knowing where he was going.*

Hebrews 11:8

Incredible—he didn't even know where he was going at first. This was an older man who had lived a long life in a famed city, and he was called to leave the land, his relatives, and everything he'd known to follow God. It couldn't have been easy. In fact, Abram didn't leave *all* his relatives—he took his wife, of course, but also his father and nephew. And he didn't go quite as far as God intended, at least initially. The group settled about halfway, in Haran, which was still in Mesopotamia. When Abram's father died, God called him again—and soon renamed him Abraham. At that point, he settled in Canaan (see Genesis 12:1–5).

Maybe in taking his father and nephew and settling in Haran, Abraham was clinging to the former things—at least a little. We can certainly understand. Imagine leaving everything you've known, including your relatives, to go to a place you've never been. For some of us, moving a few miles from one town to the next would be a hardship.

Abraham wasn't perfect. He would father a child with his wife's maid, thinking that was the only way to fulfill God's promise to give him a son, since Abraham's wife, Sarah, was old. But we don't have to be perfect or understand perfectly—or even obey perfectly—to follow God. Abraham had a *heart* to follow and to cling to God. He left a land that worshipped other gods and he became the spiritual father of descendants worldwide who belong to the true and living God. Only God can transform a life in that way. We see that transforming power when we follow and cling.

And who could talk about letting go to follow and cling without marveling at Ruth? Ruth was born and raised in the land of Moab, where her people also worshipped other gods. But she met and married Mahlon, an Israelite whose family had settled in Moab to escape a famine in Israel. For ten years, Ruth lived with Mahlon and his family—his mother, Naomi, and his brother Chilion and his wife, Orpah. But Mahlon and his brother died, leaving only the women. When Naomi learned that the famine had ended, she decided it was time to return to the land of Israel.

Both Ruth and Orpah started on the journey, but Naomi urged them to return to their old homes in Moab. They refused, weeping, insisting that they would go to Israel with their mother-in-law. Naomi reminded them what was at stake: they were unmarried and without sons, and there was no way Naomi could be of help to them. The path that made the most sense, the one with the best outlook for them, was to stay in their own land.

Orpah took Naomi's counsel and returned "to her people and her gods" (Ruth 1:15).

"But Ruth clung to her" (Ruth 1:14).

Don't you love it? It's our word *dabaq*. Ruth held fast to her mother-in-law. But the clinging wasn't merely a hug. It was this pledge:

> *"Do not urge me to leave you or turn back from following you; for where you go, I will go, and where you lodge, I will lodge. Your people shall be my people, and your God, my God. Where you die, I will die, and there I will be buried. Thus may the LORD do to me, and worse, if anything but death parts you and me."*
>
> Ruth 1:16–17

I want to jump out of my seat every time I read that. Don't stop me from following! Don't stop me from letting go of all that I've clung to my entire life—the things of Moab, the people of Moab, the gods of Moab. Ruth's heart was set and determined to follow not just Naomi but Naomi's *God*. In clinging to Naomi, Ruth was clinging to the true and living God.

I hope we don't read these accounts and reckon that this was easy. It couldn't have been easy for Ruth to relocate to a distant land, not knowing how the people might receive her. It's interesting that when she and Naomi reached the land of Israel, the Bible begins to refer to her as "Ruth the Moabitess," signaling that she was different. And that fact didn't escape her. Surely, she looked different and felt different, and was taken aback when Boaz, a wealthy landowner, treated her with kindness as she gleaned in his fields. She said to him, "Why have I found favor in your sight that you should take notice of me, since I am a foreigner?" (Ruth 2:10).

And yet it was God who had bestowed her with favor. She had left everything for Him, and He had gone before her, making the rough places smooth. He had even caused her decision to "follow and cling" to go forth as a testimony—a testimony which had reached Boaz and moved him. He said to her:

> *"All that you have done for your mother-in-law after the death of your husband has been fully reported to me, and how you left your father and your mother and the land of your birth, and came to a people that you did not previously know. May the LORD reward your work, and your wages be full from the LORD, the God of Israel, under whose wings you have come to seek refuge."*
>
> Ruth 2:11–12

As with both Abram and the fishermen who followed Jesus, God had a plan for Ruth before the foundation of the world. In leaving Moab, she had let go of what seemed her best opportunity to marry and have children—and she was okay with that. Knowing, following, and clinging to God were more important to her. But, as God would have it, she ended up marrying an Israelite, Boaz. They would have a son, Obed. And Obed would become the father of Jesse, who would become the father of David. And David would become king. From the standpoint of eternity, she is no longer known as "Ruth the Moabitess." In the New Testament, she is listed simply as "Ruth"—in the lineage of Jesus!

Abraham and Ruth left everything they'd ever known in order to follow and cling to God. And in His faithfulness, He took their offering—life itself—and transformed it for His glory.

What are you clinging to that it's time to let go of? Ask the Lord, and let Him whisper the answer in your heart. It may not be easy to let go, but He gives grace. And His plans for you are far better.

Clinging to the Calling Rather Than God

Sometimes the scenario is very different from the ones above. Someone may be following God and clinging to Him, and God may be transforming that person's life and using her for His glory. But as God uses that individual, she begins to enjoy those aspects of the calling that go beyond simple love and service. There may be attention. Power over others. Followers. She begins to build her own realm rather than the kingdom of Christ. In our Christian culture, this is a constant temptation. We know the enemy doesn't want us clinging to God, and he devises strategies to draw us away. A clever tactic is to corrupt the very thing God has called us to do—by making it about us.

As a result, though God has put us in a particular position, we don't trust Him with the outcome. Instead, we fear that what He's given might be taken away. The status we've enjoyed might be gone. So we protect our "platform," at all cost. We make choices that cater to our own desires. Soon, we are clinging to the calling rather than clinging to God.

Daniel faced this sort of test. He lived during the time that Jeremiah had prophesied about—that time when King Nebuchadnezzar of Babylon conquered Jerusalem as judgment for sin. As a youth, Daniel was taken captive to Babylon. But he was determined to cling to God.

When Nebuchadnezzar ordered that the best of the noble youth from Israel be educated for three years before entering his service, Daniel was among them. The king even dictated the food and wine that these youths were to consume, a menu that went against the dietary guidelines God had given Israel. Thus, "Daniel made up his mind that he would not defile himself with the king's choice food or with the wine which he drank" (Daniel 1:8).

Speaking for himself and three others—Shadrach, Meshach, and Abed-nego—Daniel sought permission from the head commander to have nothing but vegetables and water. It was a dangerous request, since the king would have the commander's head if those youth began to look weak compared to the others. But God gave them favor, and the request was granted.

God gave the four young men an appearance that was *better* than that of the youths who ate the king's choice food. And at the end of the training period, when the king spoke with all of the youth, *not one* was found like Daniel, Shadrach, Meshach, and Abed-nego. Incredibly, "as for every matter of wisdom and understanding about which the king consulted them, he found them ten times better than all the magicians and conjurers who were in all his realm" (Daniel 1:20).

God had a calling on the lives of these young Israelites. He intended to use them for His glory. As for Daniel, God gave him the ability to interpret King Nebuchadnezzar's dreams, and the king promoted him—Daniel became ruler over the entire province of Babylon. He was so influential that at his request, the king also appointed Shadrach, Meshach and Abed-nego to positions of governance in Babylon (Daniel 2:48–49).

God continued to use Daniel mightily when Nebuchadnezzar's successor Belshazzar, became king. At a great feast, Belshazzar brought out golden goblets that had been taken from the temple in Jerusalem. The people were drinking wine from them and praising their gods, when suddenly they saw a mysterious hand appear near a plastered wall of the palace, tracing out a message with its fingers. The king was frightened and sought to know what the message meant, yet none of his wise men could interpret the words. But the queen remembered Daniel, and how he'd interpreted Nebuchadnezzar's dreams.

Belshazzar summoned Daniel, promising royal gifts as well as authority as third ruler in the kingdom if he could interpret the message. Daniel replied, "Keep your gifts for yourself, or give your rewards to someone else; however I will read the inscription to the king and make the interpretation known to him" (Daniel 5:17). He did interpret it—a message from God that the king hadn't humbled himself, and that his kingdom would be given to the Medes and Persians. That same night Belshazzar was slain, but not before he bestowed gifts on Daniel and made him the third ruler in the kingdom (Daniel 5:29).

Daniel had found favor with two Babylonian kings who'd given him high positions in government. And with the Medes and Persians now in power, he distinguished himself all the more: he was one of three commissioners in charge of the whole kingdom. But King Darius decided to give Daniel sole authority over the kingdom because "he possessed an extraordinary spirit" (Daniel 6:3).

Other officials, jealous of Daniel's power, wanted to take him down. They couldn't find a valid accusation against him, but they knew Daniel to be a praying man—so they persuaded the king to establish a law that no one could pray to anyone but the king for thirty days. Violators would be cast into the lions' den.

His real enemy was working overtime. In Satan's view, Daniel—now an older man—had been following after God and clinging to Him for far too long. And he'd been blessed for far too long. What should've been a miserable existence as a slave in Babylon had turned into decades of power and influence in a foreign land. It needed to end. By the enemy's calculation, Daniel was in a no-win situation. He had a powerful position in the most powerful empire on earth. He had favor and influence. Surely he would cling to that. But if he went against the law and prayed, thus ending his life, all the better.

Daniel didn't cling to the things of this world—not power and position, not glory or fame or reputation, not even his own life. Daniel clung to God, the One who'd given him the fame and power and position. What was Daniel's reaction when he heard about this new law?

Now when Daniel knew that the document was signed, he entered his house (now in his roof chamber he had windows open toward Jerusalem); and he continued kneeling on his knees three times a day, praying and giving thanks before his God, as he had been doing previously.

Daniel 6:10

The conspirators spied him out and reported it to the king. Darius was distressed—he liked Daniel—yet bound by law to throw Daniel to the lions. But get this: the king said to Daniel, "Your God *whom you constantly serve* will Himself deliver you" (Daniel 6:16, emphasis added). Again, when the king awoke at dawn and hurried to see about Daniel, he said, "Daniel, servant of the living God, has your God, *whom you constantly serve*, been able to deliver you from the lions?" (Daniel 6:20).

When you cling to God, it's obvious. It's not that you're *telling* everyone; it just shows in your life, your choices, your integrity, and your devotion. Daniel was a living witness to the power of serving the true and living God, and he made an impact on this pagan king as he had with the kings before him. Importantly, the kings *knew* that what set Daniel apart was nothing in himself—it was his God.

Daniel told Darius, "My God sent His angel and shut the lions' mouths, and they have not harmed me" (Daniel 6:22). The king brought Daniel back out of the den, threw Daniel's accusers in (they were promptly crushed by the lions), and issued another decree—that all were to fear and tremble before Daniel's God (Daniel 6:26).

Daniel is an amazing example of what it means to cling to *God*, not to the calling or the ministry or the trappings of ministry. Daniel held those things loosely, not caring if he received blessing or had it stripped away. He didn't even hold tightly to his own life. Daniel would cling to God, and trust Him with the outcome.

But what about Queen Esther? Remember her?

Esther lived under Persian reign also, roughly a century after Daniel, and she faced a dire situation as well. She'd been raised by her cousin Mordecai, who was descended from Israelites who'd been taken captive from Jerusalem. And Esther rose to a place of prominence in the Persian kingdom. How? King Ahasuerus, angry with his wife, had conducted a search for a new queen—and out of all the young women considered, Esther had found favor with him. She was crowned for the royal position.

Soon, though, Esther received horrible news: Haman, one of the king's highest officers, had persuaded the king that the Jewish people were a threat to his kingdom because they refused to obey his laws. Haman had gotten the king to sign a decree that said all of the Jewish people would be destroyed on a particular day. Mordecai had put on sackcloth and ashes in the city square, a public sign of mourning, and informed Esther of the decree, telling her that she needed to go to the king and plead for her people.

There was one slight problem—you didn't just waltz in to see the king. You had to be summoned. And if you attempted to waltz in without a summons, you would be put to death unless the king held forth his golden scepter. Esther related this fact to Mordecai, thinking it would settle the matter. *No, thank you—not risking my life.* Besides, in her mind, Esther was safe with respect to the decree. She'd never revealed to the king that she was Jewish. She could continue clinging to her life of royal luxury.

Mordecai sent her another message, a stinging one:

> *"Do not imagine that you in the king's palace can escape any more than all the Jews. For if you remain silent at this time, relief and deliverance will arise for the Jews from another place and you and your father's house will perish. And who knows whether you have not attained royalty for such a time as this?"*

> Esther 4:13–14

At that, Esther relented, calling for a three-day fast among the Jews in the capital city, after which she would go in to the king. "If I perish, I perish," she said (Esther 4:16).

Mordecai's wisdom is fitting for us all. Whatever position we attain, however large or small, is given by God for the times in which we live—for His purpose. It was God who, in His sovereignty, had given Esther favor that made the king delight in her and name her queen. It was God who had placed her in the midst of riches and handmaidens. But not for her to cling to and protect. Not for her own comfort, enjoyment, and security. No, it was so that she could be used by Him to thwart the destruction of an entire race of people. Her people. God's people.

When Esther clung to God, through prayer and fasting, she saw God move in amazing ways. The king was gracious when she approached him, and held forth his golden scepter. And at a feast prepared for the king, when Esther revealed her heritage and pleaded for her people, he rose instantly to her defense. Haman was hanged on the gallows, and the Jewish people were victorious.

Clinging to God is a constant journey. Our Lord calls us to deny ourselves, take up our cross, and follow. And we belong to Him, so our hearts resonate with this. We are wholly on board, in theory. But when we get that specific call—to leave a job, a place or a ministry position, to let go of a long-held dream—our hearts are tested. Will we truly follow? Will we truly trust God and cling to Him?

And what if we leave something that's important to us, embark on a faith-walk with God, and find that He's using us greatly? What if, like Daniel, we're given power and position in this world, or a ministry that, in the eyes of others, makes us celebrities? Would we cling to it? Or would we steadfastly cling to God, even if He told us to walk away?

Since we live in a fallen world and struggle with flesh that enjoys the things of this world, our hearts will be tested constantly. But we *can* remain steadfast by the power of the Holy Spirit, as we keep our eyes fixed on Jesus, our supreme example in denying self. Jesus did not cling even to His full glory as eternal God, but instead "emptied Himself, taking the form of a bond-servant, and being made in the likeness of men" (Philippians 2:7). During His stay on earth, Jesus clung to the Father, praying to Him constantly, accomplishing His will—all the way to death on the cross.

For this reason also, God highly exalted Him, and bestowed on Him the name which is above every name, so that at the name of Jesus every knee will bow, of those who are in heaven and on earth and under the earth,

and that every tongue will confess that Jesus Christ is Lord, to the glory of
God the Father.

Philippians 2:9–11

It is in this powerful name—the name of Jesus—that we sacrifice, follow, and cling. When we focus on Him and what He's done for us, our hearts are encouraged to deny self and live for Him. Nothing in this world compares to the hope we have in Christ. Nothing compares to the glory to come. As we cling, we store up eternal treasures in heaven and experience the power of a transformed life here on earth—to the glory of our Lord.

10

The Strong and Courageous in Clinging

He grew up, physically and spiritually, under Moses. As a youth, Joshua was at Moses's side, attending to him, learning from him. He saw firsthand the relationship Moses had with God.

Just picture young Joshua, present in this grand scene: "So Moses arose with Joshua his servant, and Moses went up to the mountain of God" (Exodus 24:13). All of the elders of Israel had been told to remain where they were. Joshua alone went up, and waited forty days and forty nights as Moses received commandments from God.

For the rest of the people of Israel, this was an interminably long time. They said to Aaron, Moses's brother, "Come, make us a god who will go before us; as for this Moses, the man who brought us up from the land of Egypt, we do not know what has become of him" (Exodus 32:1). Aaron fashioned a golden calf from the people's jewelry, and then built an altar for it. The people didn't need to wonder much longer what had become of Moses, because he entered the camp as they danced and sang before their offerings to the idol.

Joshua saw the idol worship, and the response of Moses. In anger, Moses threw down the tablets of stone God had given him, shattering them at the base of the mountain. He burned the golden calf, ground it to powder, and scattered it over the people's drinking water. And he called on "whoever is for the Lord" (Exodus 32:26) to follow God's command to kill the disobedient—three thousand were slain in judgment for their sin. But Joshua also saw Moses interceding for the people the next day, asking God to forgive them their sin.

In Moses, Joshua had a model of what it looks like to cling to God. In the other people around him, Joshua had a vivid illustration of what it looks like *not* to cling. He would soon find himself smack in the middle, as he faced a test as to what he himself would do.

Joshua was one of twelve spies sent by Moses to see what the land God had promised was like. After forty days in Canaan, the spies returned and confirmed that it was indeed as fruitful as God had said—flowing with milk and honey. But the people in the land were big and strong, so strong that the spies felt like grasshoppers in comparison. As a result, ten of the spies concluded, "We are not able to go up against the people, for they are too strong for us" (Numbers 13:31).

And based on the report of these ten, all the people wept and cried out, saying, "Why is the Lord bringing us into this land, to fall by the sword? Our wives and our little ones will become plunder; would it not be better for us to return to Egypt?" (Numbers 14:3). Yes, they decided. They would appoint a leader and return to the land from which God had mightily delivered them.

But two of the spies—Joshua and Caleb—had a different report. The land was exceedingly good, they said, and God would bring them into the land and give it to them. "Only do not rebel against the Lord; and do not fear the people of the land, for they will be our prey. Their protection has been removed from them, and the Lord is with us; do not fear them" (Numbers 14:9).

Joshua and Caleb were clinging! And they knew the power in clinging. Clinging to God meant they didn't need to fear, no matter how big and strong the enemy was. Clinging to God meant courage. They could go into the land because it was God who would go before them and give it to them. Hadn't they already seen great signs and wonders on their behalf? They simply needed to trust and believe.

But Joshua and Caleb weren't persuasive. The people were ready to stone them.

God had had enough. He appeared in the peoples' midst and pronounced judgment against them. For forty years, that entire generation of Israelites would wander in the wilderness and die there—all except Joshua and Caleb. The next generation would be the people to enter into the land. And who would lead them? Joshua.

Moses passed the mantle himself. He told Joshua, the man who had followed him from his youth,

"Be strong and courageous, for you shall go with this people into the land which the LORD has sworn to their fathers to give them, and you shall give it to them as an inheritance. The LORD is the one who goes ahead of you; He will be with you. He will not fail you or forsake you. Do not fear, or be dismayed."

Deuteronomy 31:7–8

Then, in the presence of Moses, God Himself commissioned Joshua, saying again, "**Be strong and courageous**, for you shall bring the sons of Israel into the land which I swore to them, and I will be with you" (Deuteronomy 31:23).

In both verses, did you notice what was tied to being strong and courageous? *God will be with you.* Moses promised it, and God said it in His own words. Knowing God was near, that He was *with* him, would bolster Joshua's ability to be strong and courageous.

But then Moses died. Oh, the grief and sadness Joshua must have felt. He'd been by the side of Moses for decades, serving him, even soldiering for him. When Aaron and Hur kept Moses's arms lifted so that Israel could be victorious against Amalek, it was Joshua who led the charge on the battlefield.

Always, Joshua had looked to Moses and followed Moses. And he had watched as God spoke to Moses. Now Moses was gone, and it would be natural for Joshua to feel low. But God had a word for Joshua: "Moses My servant is dead; now therefore arise, cross this Jordan, you and all this people, to the land which I am giving to them" (Joshua 1:2). And God said this: "Just as I have been with Moses, I will be with you; I will not fail you or forsake you" (Joshua 1:5).

Such tenderness from God. Such intimacy. Moses was gone, but God Himself would be with Joshua *just as* He'd been with Moses. Now that was saying something! Joshua had clung to God while spying out the land and trying to convince the Israelites to obey God and believe His promises. Now, God reassured him that He was there for Joshua, always.

After this assurance, here is the charge that followed:

Be strong and courageous . . .

Oh, it's my prayer that we would get this deep into our hearts. When God is with us, when we're dwelling intimately with Him, how can we *not* be strong and courageous in whatever He's calling us to do? How can we not face trials and tests with strength and courage? How can we not trust and believe that He will establish His promises in Christ Jesus toward us?

"Be strong and courageous" was not just for Joshua. It's for all of us in Christ. Yet I love the fact that God knows our human hearts, that we need to be told such things more than once. Twice before Moses died, Joshua had been instructed to "be strong and courageous." Now, God would repeat it *three* more times.

"Be strong and courageous, for you shall give this people possession of the land."

Joshua 1:6

"Only be strong and very courageous."

Joshua 1:7

"Have I not commanded you? **Be strong and courageous!** *Do not tremble or be dismayed, for the LORD your God is with you wherever you go."*

Joshua 1:9

But that's not all God said. He told Joshua that he would prosper and have success only if he meditated day and night on the law that Moses commanded, and was careful to obey it. This is exciting, because I *know* Joshua was front and center when Moses said this to that next generation of Israelites about to enter the Promised Land:

"You shall fear the LORD your God; you shall serve Him and **cling to Him,** *and you shall swear by His name."*

Deuteronomy 10:20

And this:

"You shall follow the LORD your God and fear Him; and you shall keep His commandments, listen to His voice, serve Him, and **cling to Him."**

Deuteronomy 13:4

And this:

"For if you are careful to keep all this commandment which I am commanding you to do, to love the LORD your God, to walk in all his ways and **hold fast** *[same word as "cling"] to Him; then the LORD will drive out all these nations from before you."*

Deuteronomy 11:22–23

Joshua knew that his prosperity and success lay in clinging to God. He was about to go into the land and conquer, the very thing ten spies said couldn't be done. Those ten weren't clinging to God. And when we're not clinging to God, we are overcome with fear and overwhelmed by a focus on our limited selves. The spies were like grasshoppers compared to the people in the Promised Land—but what about God? If their eyes had been fixed on Him and His strength, they could have gone forth in His power, just as Joshua did. They, too, could have been strong and courageous.

Joshua clung to God and, as a result, led Israel to conquer nations and occupy the land God had promised. And when Joshua was old and Israel had rest from its enemies, he didn't say, "Well, we have peace. No more need to be strong and courageous. I can stop clinging now." He knew that the people's continued prosperity lay in holding fast, always, to God: "But you are to **cling** to the LORD your God, as you have done to this day" (Joshua 23:8).

I love that clinging to God leads to strength and courage. God shows up in such unexpected ways when His people cling. We see it throughout the Bible, and I find myself often returning to those passages. Knowing that God told Joshua several times to "be strong and courageous," I'm encouraged when I read again and again about those who walked in divine strength and courage as they clung to God. Those living words tunnel deep into my marrow and transform the worry, doubt, and fear into faith that is strengthened.

You can probably tell that Joshua is one of my go-to people when I need a reminder to "be strong and courageous." David is too, especially in his battle with Goliath. But I've got two others I turn to consistently, two clinging, "strong and courageous" kings—Jehoshaphat and Hezekiah.

God Is Not Able to Deliver?

If we're honest, we sometimes entertain that thought—God is not able to deliver. Oh, He delivered us from darkness to light, but *this particular circumstance* is just too big. Or too painful. Or too impossible. We might pray about it, but deep down we don't expect a change. Just too many factors at work to convince us otherwise.

These are thoughts the enemy delights in. He wants us to doubt God's ability to deliver. He shoots those very thoughts into our minds, hoping we will sink in despair and give up. It's a tactic the enemy used against the children of Israel when Hezekiah was king.

The Assyrians were the leading world power. They had already taken the northern kingdom of Israel into captivity, and now they were coming against the southern kingdom of Judah. Along with a large army, the Assyrian king sent his commanders to Jerusalem, and they embarked upon an interesting strategy. They sought to dismantle the confidence Hezekiah and the people of Israel had in God. They mocked:

> *"But do not listen to Hezekiah, when he misleads you, saying, 'The LORD will deliver us.'. . . Who among all the gods of the lands have delivered their land from my hand, that the LORD should deliver Jerusalem from my hand?"*

2 Kings 18:32, 35

The Assyrian king had conquered other places and in his pride, assumed he could also take down Jerusalem. He sent a follow-up message to Hezekiah, taunting once more: "Do not let your God in whom you trust deceive you saying, 'Jerusalem will not be given into the hand of the king of Assyria'" (2 Kings 19:10). The gods of the other nations couldn't deliver them. Why would Hezekiah think *his* God could deliver?

The enemy attacks our thoughts in the same way. Why would we trust God to deliver? He'll even remind us of other instances in which God *didn't* deliver, as an indictment of His strength or faithfulness. But we don't know why God chooses to deliver in some instances and not others. His ways are higher, and we can't begin to understand His purposes. But we *do* know that He's *able* to deliver—and that He's faithful. By faith we cling to Him and stand on the truth of His Word, even when the situation looks impossible. Especially when it looks impossible.

That's what Hezekiah did. The Assyrian king didn't know whom he was dealing with. This was Hezekiah's reputation before God:

> *For he **clung** to the LORD; he did not depart from following Him, but kept His commandments, which the LORD had commanded Moses. And the LORD was with him; wherever he went he prospered.*

2 Kings 18:6–7

Did you see that? It's the same formula for prosperity as we saw with Joshua—clinging to God, following Him, keeping His commandments. What did it look like for Hezekiah to cling to God in the face of those taunts from the enemy? He took the threatening letter, went to the house of the Lord, and spread it before God.

I *love* that. Hezekiah could have taken the letter home and focused on it, reading the challenge over and over, stoking his own fear. Instead, he took it to God. Of course God knew about the letter and what it said, but this one act was strength-building. Taking the threat-filled letter to the house of the Lord put it into perspective. Did it amount to anything in light of the King of Glory? No!

Hezekiah started his prayer with praise. The Assyrian king had minimized God, putting Him on the same level as the gods of other nations. So Hezekiah praised God as the Most High: "O LORD, the God of Israel, who are enthroned above the cherubim, You are the God, You alone, of all the kingdoms of the earth. You have made heaven and earth" (2 Kings 19:15).

When we pray in this way, we remind ourselves that there is none like God. He is maker of heaven and earth, and nothing that concerns us is beyond His knowledge or control. Praise checks our worries and fears and lifts our focus. Praise lifts our courage.

Then Hezekiah addressed that letter:

"Incline Your ear, O LORD, and hear; open Your eyes, O LORD, and see; and listen to the words of Sennacherib, which he has sent to reproach the living God. Truly, O LORD, the kings of Assyria have devastated the nations and their lands and have cast their gods into the fire, for they were not gods but the work of men's hands, wood and stone. So they have destroyed them. Now, O LORD our God, I pray, deliver us from his hand that all the kingdoms of the earth may know that You alone, O LORD, are God."

2 Kings 19:16–19

That's how we cling in the face of a great challenge. We lay it out before God and give it to Him, acknowledging that He is well able to handle it. And we pray for Him to deliver, for His own glory, honor, and praise. We pray in faith, yet we are also mindful, as Jesus taught, to pray that the Lord's will be done. We won't be delivered from every circumstance in the way we might like. But we can trust that the Lord will work all things together for our good (Romans 8:28). And always, we can stand strong and courageous, prospering despite the circumstances, because our eternity is sure.

How did God respond to the matter with Assyria? Sennacherib and his military leaders had boasted of their might and the lands they had conquered, yet they failed to realize that it was all according to God's sovereign plan and purpose. As for Jerusalem, the king of Assyria wouldn't so much as shoot an arrow there. God said, "I will defend this city to save it for My own sake and for my servant David's sake" (2 Kings 19:34). That same night, the angel of the Lord struck dead every man in the Assyrian camp.

When the enemy whispers his lie that God is not able to deliver, *cling* to God all the more. Be strong and courageous. Our God is mighty in power.

The Battle Is Not Yours

When we think about being strong and courageous, we may think that we have to muster the heroism ourselves. Just the thought is tiresome, especially in the midst of a difficult trial. But it's encouraging to remember that we stand in *God's* strength. "Finally, be strong in the Lord, and in the strength of His might" (Ephesians 6:10). We clothe ourselves in *His* armor. "Put on the full armor of God, so that you will be able to stand firm against the schemes of the devil" (Ephesians 6:11). And *then* we fight? Well, actually, He does that too.

David understood that truth when he fought Goliath. He told the giant that the Lord would deliver, not by sword or spear, "for the battle is the LORD's and He will give you into our hands" (1 Samuel 17:47). Hundreds of years later, King Jehoshaphat would learn this powerful truth, when the Moabites and Ammonites came to make war against him. When he got word, Scripture says, "Jehoshaphat was afraid . . ." (2 Chronicles 20:3). I'm thankful for the reminder that these were real people with real emotions. That moment we receive news of something big and terrible, that news will most certainly dominate our focus. The only question is for how long.

For Jehoshaphat, it wasn't long at all. He moved immediately to a clinging posture. This is the full sentence in 2 Chronicles 20:3: "Jehoshaphat was afraid and turned his attention to seek the LORD." Yes! Don't give fear time to fester and grow. Don't give it a voice in setting strategy and a course of action. Turn from fear, and seek the Lord.

Jehoshaphat proclaimed a fast throughout Judah and called the people together for prayer. Like Hezekiah, he drew their focus away from earthly dread to God Almighty, high and lifted up:

"O LORD, the God of our fathers, are You not God in the heavens? And are You not ruler over all the kingdoms of the nations? Power and might are in Your hand so that no one can stand against You."

2 Chronicles 20:6

"Strong and courageous" begins to course through your veins when you remind yourself of these truths. And it's absolutely true—power and might are in God's hand. *No one* can stand against Him.

Jehoshaphat reminded God of His promises toward His people, that He had given them this land from which their enemies were now trying to drive them. Then Jehoshaphat uttered words that I often repeat:

"For we are powerless before this great multitude who are coming against us; nor do we know what to do, but our eyes are on You."

2 Chronicles 20:12

That's the strength in clinging. I've got nothing, Lord—nothing for this great trial, this immense storm, this relentless attack. Zero power in this situation. And I don't know what to do, except to keep my eyes on You, the One with all power.

As Jehoshaphat and the people waited, the Lord sent this message through one of the men in the assembly: "Do not fear or be dismayed because of this great multitude, for the battle is not yours but God's" (2 Chronicles 20:15). And he told them they need not fight: "Stand and see the salvation of the LORD on your behalf. . . . Do not fear or be dismayed; tomorrow go out to face them, for the LORD is with you" (20:17).

The next morning they went out to meet the enemy. But Jehoshaphat didn't put soldiers in front—that's where he placed *worshippers*, those who sang and praised God. They led the army into battle, with this war cry: "Give thanks to the LORD, for His lovingkindness is everlasting" (2 Chronicles 20:21).

Picture it, over and over as they marched:

> Give thanks to the LORD, for His lovingkindness is everlasting!
> Give thanks to the LORD, for His lovingkindness is everlasting!
> Give thanks to the LORD, for His lovingkindness is everlasting!

They were giving thanks before they saw the outcome. They were praising God's lovingkindness, not based on a circumstance, but because it's everlasting, no matter the circumstance. They were declaring to us all that clinging to God through prayer and praise brings us strength and courage. Every time I read this story, I want to shout.

And look what the Bible says next: "When they began singing and praising, the LORD set ambushes against the sons of Ammon, Moab, and Mount Seir, who had come against Judah; so they were routed" (2 Chronicles 20:22). *The LORD set . . . He* did it. True to His word, His people didn't have to fight.

I return to this passage time and again, but not because I face a physical army coming against me or I expect God to show up in such an amazing way in every single circumstance. I return to this passage because we are *all* in a spiritual war—with principalities arrayed against us. We face trying circumstances which bring worry and fear, and Jehoshaphat is a powerful example of what to do in the face of those circumstances—turn to seek the Lord, pray, fast, trust—*cling*. God says to us as well, "Do not fear or be dismayed, for I am with you." He wants us also to be assured that He's the one who fights for us. I return to this passage because this is our God!

And truly, we ought to look for God to show up in a very real and powerful way in our lives. When I'm in despair and peace comes over me, He's shown up in a powerful way. When I have no idea what to do in the face of a challenge, and a pathway opens up, He's shown up in a powerful way. When I give Him thanks and praise in the midst of tears, and I'm flooded with strength to keep on keepin' on, He's shown up in a powerful way. As was the case with Jehoshaphat, the enemy— the true enemy—has been routed. God shows us in infinite ways that power and might are in His hand, and no one can stand against Him.

Strong and Courageous Witnesses

Clinging to God is not a formula we follow so that we get whatever we want. No, we cling out of our love for God, out of our desire to know Him and walk with Him. We cling because we want His ways to be our ways and His thoughts, our thoughts. We cling because He loved us before we loved Him, so much so that He sent His Son to save us. And we cling because Jesus is our Lord and Savior, our all, the One for whom and unto whom we live.

In clinging, we can be strong and courageous because ultimately, we have nothing to fear. We serve an eternal King who will come again in power and glory. And we will live eternally with Him. Our current lives are but a vapor, and whatever trouble we endure is momentary, even "light" compared to the "eternal weight of glory" that it's producing (2 Corinthians 4:17).

The funny thing about clinging is that it begins with a place of intimacy, yet it extends abundantly to others. We are becoming more like

Jesus, which means we are spreading the "sweet aroma of the knowledge of Him in every place" (2 Corinthians 2:14). People see that something is different about us. Through hardships, we have hope—joy, even. We live with purpose. We have an eternal perspective, so that we are not in utter despair when life crumbles around us.

And we are "not ashamed of the gospel, for it is the power of God for salvation to everyone who believes" (Romans 1:16). We can be strong and courageous in sharing Christ, as we are called to do, so that others can not only be saved but know the freedom and joy of dwelling intimately with the Lord. Clinging to God makes us a vessel through which others learn to cling to God and impact the world.

Yes. That's what *you* will do when you cling. You will impact the sphere of the world in which God has placed you.

"He who abides in Me and I in him, he bears much fruit, for apart from Me you can do nothing."

John 15:5

Study Guide

SESSION 1: CLING

What to Do

- If you have the *Cling* DVD, watch the first video.
- If you do not have the video, read the transcript below.
- Think through and discuss the questions that follow.

I am so excited to walk with you through a study of my book *Cling*. We're going to talk about what it looks like to cling to God. We'll even discuss what keeps us from clinging to God. We're going to explore the beautiful truth that God already knows you intimately. And He's put in place everything you need to know Him.

We long for intimate relationships in our lives. Yet, in spite of our deep longing for such relationships, all too often there's a void.

I've been there. I've had seasons in life when it seemed there was no one I could talk to in a deep way. I've been heartbroken when relationships haven't been what I hoped they would be.

Why do we do this? Because we have a deep longing for intimacy that is not meant to be satisfied by people. Our desire for intimacy—the kind that reaches down to the core—was put there by God, and He's the only One who can satisfy it.

I didn't grow up in a Christian household. My parents divorced when I was four, and I was raised primarily by my mother, who loved me and cared for me. But we hardly ever went to church. So I didn't know God—I didn't even know much about God.

But, going back to early childhood, I had this longing for intimacy. And in particular, I have vivid memories of wanting a closer relationship with my father. I loved my dad, and I loved being around my dad—so I'd get excited when we would make plans to get together. But when those plans didn't work out, I'd be so disappointed. As a little girl I'd wonder, *Do I matter?* Because I couldn't feel the closeness that I wanted to feel.

As I got older, I tried to fill that void. It was never a conscious thing, but looking back, something in me wanted to feel close to someone. I wanted to matter. That's what enticed me about relationships with men—the intimacy it would bring. Or so I thought. In reality, it left my soul an even more fractured mess.

But at twenty-three, I met Bill. We married when I was twenty-six, and now, more than two decades later, I'm as convinced as ever that he is a gift.

But spouses can't be all things to us. They can't fill our every void. As much of a gift as Bill was, I needed more than Bill.

I needed the Lord. And a year into my marriage, the Lord graciously drew me to Himself. I gave my life to Jesus—and from a spiritual standpoint, everything changed. I became a new creation. I was living in a new kingdom. I was blessed with every spiritual blessing. I had eternal life.

And I had a relationship with Jesus. I knew that. But what I didn't realize was that I could have a deep, abiding, day-to-day relationship. I didn't know I could grow to know Jesus as a friend, to talk to Him about *anything*, to dwell with Him, and to hear from Him.

In Deuteronomy 10:20, Moses says to God's people: "You shall fear the LORD your God; you shall serve Him and **cling** to Him, and you shall swear by His name." And again in Deuteronomy 13:4: "You shall follow the LORD your God and fear Him; and you shall keep His commandments, listen to His voice, serve Him, and **cling** to Him."

Cling. I love that word. From the first time I heard it, it became a prayer that I've prayed through the years: "Lord, help me to cling to you." And this is why I love it: the other commandments in those verses from Deuteronomy can be satisfied from a distance. Serving God, fearing God, and keeping His commandments can all be done from a distance. You can even follow from a distance as long as you're headed in the same direction. But clinging puts you in God's face. You're glued to Him. It's personal. Intimate.

The word in Hebrew is *dabaq.* It means "cling," "cleave," or "keep close." Your Bible might say, "hold fast."

This is what God *wants* from us—a close, intimate relationship, where we are one with Him.

And what's exciting is that there's a New Testament counterpart to **cling**, another word I love—**abide**. In John chapter 15, Jesus gives us a beautiful word picture. He tells us that He is the vine, His Father is the vinedresser, and we are the branches. This imagery inspired us to record here in this vineyard, where we can see living vines and understand the truth of Jesus's words. Because this is what He said—it's another gracious invitation: "Abide in me, and I in you. As the branch cannot bear fruit of itself unless it abides in the vine, so neither can you unless you abide in Me."

To abide in Jesus is to be united with Him in heart and mind and will, to be *one* with Him . . . to be in an intimate relationship with Him. When we are abiding, we are clinging.

It is my prayer that this study will inspire you to accept God's gracious invitation to cling to Him—to daily choose a lifestyle of intimacy with Him. And oh, the blessing in doing so! It doesn't mean that you're living a perfect life and doing everything right—that's not even possible in this human frame. What it means is that—in the midst of our imperfect lives, in troubled and often scary times, in disappointment and heartache—you are secure, walking closely, glued to an almighty, loving, and faithful God.

CLING TO THE WORD

Read: John 15

Memorize: "You shall follow the LORD your God and fear Him; and you shall keep His commandments, listen to His voice, serve Him, and cling to Him" (Deuteronomy 13:4).

Discuss

1. Think about a person you felt was a true kindred spirit in your life. What set that person apart from others in the way you connected? Can you recall one special time when your friendship clicked and you created a wonderful memory?

2. Think of a time when you really needed someone to connect with, but you found no one. Describe what that felt like.

3. What do you think of Kim's idea that no other human can really satisfy our deepest longing? How does that concept square with the general thinking in our culture?

4. On a scale of 0 to 10, how would you rate your relationship with your father? Why? If you have positive memories, what is one of the best?

5. Name your top four things that characterize a human relationship that provides a sense of truly connecting, of sharing in a beneficial way.

6. After Kim was married, she also experienced a spiritual blessing. Describe in your own words what she meant when she says she prayed and "gave [her] life to Jesus"?

7. Contrast the idea of having a really good friend and knowing Jesus Christ. What might be some differences between those two relationships?

8. Think of the word *cling*. What are this word's positive implications in a relationship? Can *cling* be negative as well?

9. From what Kim has said so far, put together a good definition of the word *cling* as it relates to a person's relationship with God.

10. As you think of the idea of abiding with Jesus in a new, fresh way—of clinging to Him as never before—what most excites you?

What to Do Before Session 2

• Read the introduction, chapter 1, and chapter 2.

SESSION 2: TRUST

What to Do

- In the book, review the introduction, chapter 1, and chapter 2.
- If you have the *Cling* DVD, watch the second video.
- Think through and discuss the questions that follow.

CLING TO THE WORD

Read: Exodus 13:17–22, 14:1–31

Memorize: "Trust in the LORD with all your heart and do not lean on your own understanding. In all your ways acknowledge Him, and He will make your paths straight" (Proverbs 3:5–6).

Discuss

Video

1. What do you recall of the contrast between being dead spiritually and coming alive at salvation? Or was your salvation so early in life you can't remember a difference?

2. What are some things people say about matters of faith when they know a lot *about* God but don't know Him personally?

3. In your life, how does knowing Jesus make you feel "alive" as the apostle Paul described in Ephesians 2:4–5?

4. Inspect your heart to make sure you are truly alive in Christ—that you have been redeemed by putting your faith in Jesus's sacrifice for you.

Book Introduction

1. Kim said of the crisis with her teenager, "Lord, this is too hard!" Think of a time when you felt that way—when you did not know

how you were going to make it past a high hurdle in your life. What can you share about that experience?

2. How prepared are you for the next crisis that might come your way?

3. Think what it means that God was in control throughout the story of the Exodus: He had hardened Pharaoh's heart, and He forced Pharaoh to relent. How does that realization help as you see turmoil in high places, both in the United States and around the world?

4. Along with Kim, contemplate the word *cling* in Deuteronomy 10:20 and 13:4. What elements of her explanation stand out to you as you think of your relationship to God?

5. Write your own definition of the word *cling* as it relates to you and the Lord.

6. As valuable and essential as our human relationships are, Kim suggests they are not enough. She says there's a place deep in our souls "reserved for God alone." How do you respond to that as you think about your closest friend, your spouse, or a beloved relative?

7. If you learn to cling to God in a new and vibrant way, what areas of your life do you think will be positively affected?

Book Chapter 1

1. Put yourself in the Garden of Eden, before the Fall, viewing the remarkable things happening there. What would you most like to observe in that majestic place of perfection?

2. Think about the "Let us . . ." phrase of Genesis 1:26 and contemplate the relationship of Father, Son, and Holy Spirit from eternity past. Together they were now embarking on the creation of the world—and about to introduce humankind into their relationship. That's an amazing thing to ponder!

3. Kim states, "We were created by God to cling to Him." If that is true, what happens to us, to our lives, to our daily existence when we fail to cling—when we go off on our own?

4. Kim tells about her life before Jesus, when she didn't know she was supposed to cling to the Savior. Think of times when you have been estranged from God and unable to cling. How did that go for you?

5. Kim describes the wedge—Satan—that came between God's specially created beings (Adam and Eve) and the Creator Himself. What method did Satan use to entice Eve and Adam to break their pristine relationship with God?

6. After Adam and Eve sinned, they hid from God. In what ways do *we* try to hide from God instead of doing everything possible to run back into His arms?

7. Our first parents, Adam and Eve, were kicked out of paradise—but, by extension, so were we. What are the implications of that long-ago action for our world today? Chapter 1 of *Cling* ends with an expulsion from God's presence. Think what that would feel like as you anticipate Chapter 2.

Book Chapter 2

1. What is it about marriage—about a wedding—that is so very special? In what ways does a wedding remind us of important spiritual truths and realities?

2. Amazingly, God was guiding Kim to make right decisions even before she had come to faith in Him. What are some ways God has guided you in life, clearly giving you His direction?

3. Consider the significance of the realities Kim mentioned about all who follow Adam: we "bear the image of God" and we also "bear Adam's likeness—the crimson stain of sin." How do these truths play out in our everyday lives?

4. Do you know people who live as Kim describes, people who are deceived into thinking "they can live however they want and believe whatever they want and still enjoy an eternity of heavenly bliss"? Have you ever thought that way yourself?

5. As Kim suggests, read the words of John 3:16 again, and let them reach deep into your soul. Examine the verse line by line to get the full effect.

6. When Kim speaks of being "re-created in Christ," she says "it's as if God rewinds back to the beginning," specifically Genesis 1:26. How can that concept provide a new exhilaration in your faith— even if you have been a believer for a long time? What freedom does that give you to think of yourself as being "freed from the power of darkness and sin"? How does it help you cling to the Savior?

7. Picture yourself clinging to Jesus—standing with Him arm in arm, basking in His love and power. How different do your problems appear when you are by Jesus's side?

What to Do Before Session 3

- Read chapter 3 and chapter 4.

SESSION 3: DELIGHT

What to Do

- In the book, review chapter 3 and chapter 4.
- If you have the *Cling* DVD, watch the third video.
- Think through and discuss the questions that follow.

CLING TO THE WORD

Read: Psalm 25:1–6

Memorize: "His delight is in the law of the LORD, and in His law he meditates day and night" (Psalm 1:2).

Discuss

Video

1. Have you ever contemplated the amazing truth that captured Kim's heart—that God had you in mind "before the foundation of the world"? For the Christian, what are some of the implications of this reality?

2. Kim says, "We cannot cling to God apart from clinging to His Word." How can this one simple sentence transform the way we approach the Bible?

3. Sometimes, Kim suggests, we make the Bible about us. How does this happen? How can this hinder our knowledge of God?

4. Have you ever felt that the Bible is extremely long and sometimes complicated? What do you think of Kim's suggestion that, as you read anywhere in Scripture, God will reveal Himself to you? How have you seen that happen for you as she did in Ephesians 1?

5. Have you ever thought, as some do, that the Old Testament is too distant and the New Testament is all that matters? What are

some Old Testament treasures you have gleaned that can encourage people to see its value to today's believer?

Book Chapter 3

1. In your experience, does Kim's illustration of what we might call "event-based intimacy with God" make sense? What are some of those orchestrated times when you feel close to God?

2. What is Kim saying about intimacy with God when she quotes the "before" verses such as Titus 1:2 and Ephesians 1:3–4?

3. Think what it means to say that God was proactive toward us, as 1 Peter 1:1–2 indicates. What are the implications for us as we think of intimacy with God?

4. Kim gives several biblical examples of God choosing people— Abraham, Jacob, the nation of Israel, and others. Pick an example and discuss what it must have meant to those people to know that God had so clearly selected them to do His bidding.

5. How does the reality of God's choosing us (rather than our choosing Him) help us to avoid boasting about our faith?

6. Review the moments of intimacy Jesus enjoyed with His disciples. How do His actions just before His arrest and all the terrible events that followed remind us how the Lord values relationship with His followers?

7. How does the Holy Spirit's presence in believers solidify the idea that God values intimacy with us?

Book Chapter 4

1. Discuss a time when you went from hardly knowing someone to knowing that person extensively. How did knowledge itself help that relationship?

2. In your Christian life, what were key components that helped build your knowledge of God's Word—as the Christian Women group began to do for Kim?

3. In Kim's story of wanting to know God's Word, the key word is *hunger*. "A hunger came over me that wouldn't let me rest," she said. What has given you that hunger?

4. How can a person who has been a believer for decades capture the excitement Kim experienced? How can any of us get to the place she found, where "I would pause and shake my head at the wonder of a single verse and all that it was teaching me"?

5. When she was in Israel, Kim had this prayer of David engraved on a piece of jewelry: "Show me Your ways, O LORD; teach me your paths" (Psalm 25:4). How would knowing God's ways help David to succeed over Goliath?

6. Think through the same concept in relationship to Jeremiah: How did having an intimate knowledge of God help the prophet?

7. Clinging to God helped Kim overcome her initial angst over homeschooling her kids instead of writing her next books. Have you ever faced a situation in which you thought there was no good way out—until you embraced the knowledge you had from God's Word and found a new perspective?

8. How has the reality of God's sovereignty come to your rescue when the winds of your life, as Kim says, threaten to push you off course?

What to Do Before Session 4

• Read chapter 5 and chapter 6.

SESSION 4: PRAY

What to Do

- In the book, review chapter 5 and chapter 6.
- If you have the *Cling* DVD, watch the fourth video.
- Think through and discuss the questions that follow.

CLING TO THE WORD

Read: John 15:1–8

Memorize: "Be anxious for nothing, but in everything by prayer and supplication with thanksgiving let your requests be made known to God. And the peace of God, which surpasses all comprehension, will guard your hearts and your minds in Christ Jesus" (Philippians 4:6–7).

Discuss

Video

1. In your life, do you find that when things go well you tend to drift? What are some other responses we could have when life is good?

2. When has God used a hardship in your life to draw you closer to Him? How did you feel about that?

3. Kim says, "Clinging to God during difficult times—and at any time—means clinging to truth. And it also means being fervent in prayer." God's Word and prayer will support us through those painful times when God "prunes" us. Discuss what the pruning process may be like in a Christian's life.

4. Discuss some of the impediments to prayer, and how clinging to God can help during difficult times.

5. Talk about what it might mean, as Kim mentions in concluding her video, to cultivate a lifestyle of prayer.

Book Chapter 5

1. Do you have a designated prayer place, as Kim described in her humorous explanation of her attempt at a "war room"? Share how that works for you—or doesn't.

2. Kim writes, "Talk to God. Every day. All day." Is this probable? Possible? How would this basic approach to prayer transform your relationship with God?

3. A second approach to prayer, as Kim explains, is teaming prayer with Bible study. As you examine your personal schedule, how realistic would it be to carve out time for this? Can you think of any ideas (or would you accept ideas from others) for this challenge?

4. Discuss these categories of prayer needs:

   a. Gratitude and praise: What practical ideas can spur you on toward this "beautiful symphony"?

   b. Rising flesh: When the old nature peeks out from behind the new to cause trouble, what advice from Kim can guide you to pray effectively?

   c. Tongue problems: What are two or three tongue troubles you occasionally find yourself in? What can you pray for to use your lips to represent Jesus instead of your errant thoughts?

   d. Worry: If reminding yourself of Matthew 6:34 ("Do not worry") isn't enough, how can the practice of prayer redirect your thinking in the right way?

   e. Care for others: What are the best ways to pray when the world is crashing down on people you care about?

   f. Falling into sin: We don't want it to, but sin often returns to drag us down. What prayer prompts can get us back into fellowship with God?

Book Chapter 6

1. Some people in the midst of struggle—the kind of struggle the Tates had as their son was growing up—stop clinging to God and drift away. What has helped you to stay close to God when going through a prolonged crisis?

2. In what ways did David learn that he had no choice but to cling to God? What situations have felt that way for you?

3. When David wrote, "My soul clings to You, your right hand upholds me" (Psalm 63:8), what was going on his life? How does this psalm speak to your situation now?

4. The key lesson from Job, as Kim tells his story, is this: "Job indeed took issue with God. . . . But Job did not turn his back on God." The patriarch said, "My foot has held fast to His path" (23:11), which means he kept clinging! Has anything in your life caused you nearly to slip—to leave the path of seeking God? What kept your foot from slipping?

5. Kim notes that God's teaching of Job leads us as readers to stand in awe of creation. What elements of Job 38–41 make you want to stand up and praise God?

6. What are some ways that being "called to patiently endure suffering for His sake," as Kim says, pushes us closer to God instead of away from Him—which would be the natural tendency?

What to Do Before Session 5

• Read chapter 7 and chapter 8.

SESSION 5: LOVE

What to Do

- In the book, review chapter 7 and chapter 8.
- If you have the *Cling* DVD, watch the fifth video.
- Think through and discuss the questions that follow.

CLING TO THE WORD

Read: Psalm 18:1–3

Memorize: "If you keep My commandments, you will abide in My love" (John 15:10).

Discuss

Video

1. Talk about the first time you told someone—a spouse, a parent, a sibling—"I love you." How did you know that when you heard "I love you" in return that it was the real deal?

2. Kim mentions what we might call "big sins." Without giving names, how have you seen major sins destroy lives, careers, or ministries? How does the seeming frequency of these things provide warning for our own lives?

3. Think about Kim's statement, "The beautiful truth is that a sordid past can move us to love God *more*." How can this be true?

Book Chapter 7

1. David clearly loved God, as shown by his treatment of Saul and his celebration when the ark was taken to Jerusalem. So what happened to that love when the incident with Bathsheba happened? What does David's story tell us about sin and ourselves?

2. How can we learn to see, as Kim says, that our sin is personal to God? What do you think of her startling statement, "Sin reveals a heart that despises Him and His Word"?

3. Think about this statement: "Wherever sin festers, that's an area of the heart that is not clinging to God." What happens to our relationship with God when we have a heart divided in that way?

4. The enemy, Satan, came to Eve with beguiling words that tripped her up. He came to Jesus similarly, but our Lord stood firm. In what ways does Satan come to *us* today with temptations we can only resist through clinging to God and His power?

Book Chapter 8

1. Consider the meaning of the story of the woman who washed Jesus's feet. What does that show us about the people Jesus came to save—those persons He desires to hear the gospel and come to Him in faith? Discuss how this story can change our view of sharing the gospel.

2. Review Kim's comments on sex and marriage as they relate to the idea of clinging. How can they help us explain to others that marriage is vital, and that casual sexual relations are damaging, not life-enhancing?

3. For anyone who has pursued the "immoral clinging" that Kim describes, there is the value of what Jesus said to the woman: she was forgiven. Talk about the relief and comfort that forgiveness provides, no matter what sins we've committed.

4. What do you think about Kim's statement that "the very thing in your past that causes you grief is the very thing that propels your worship"? How can we turn our past and Jesus's forgiveness of it into profound worship?

5. Imagine being the Samaritan woman and hearing Jesus reveal to *you* that He was the Messiah! What do you think she felt as she contemplated her past and realized that she was in the presence

of the hope of the world? Isn't it just like Jesus to reveal His mission to one so lost?

6. What takeaway from these two women's stories can help you cling even closer to the Savior?

What to Do Before Session 6

• Read chapter 9 and chapter 10.

SESSION 6: COURAGE

What to Do

- In the book, review chapter 9 and chapter 10.
- If you have the *Cling* DVD, watch the sixth video.
- Think through and discuss the questions that follow.

> ## CLING TO THE WORD
>
> **Read:** Deuteronomy 31:1–8
>
> **Memorize:** "Have I not commanded you? Be strong and courageous! Do not tremble or be dismayed, for the LORD your God is with you wherever you go" (Joshua 1:9).

Discuss

Video

1. There is definitely an element of excitement in jumping into thin air attached only to a harness and zip line. In what way is trusting God with our lives a little like that?

2. Why do you think Kim says, "It is somewhat comforting that Abraham didn't follow God perfectly"?

3. Kim notes the courage of the young, unwed Mary, told by an angel that she would give birth to God's own Son, Jesus. "Mary could have clung to what was comfortable—she could have clung to her own plans, she could have clung to her reputation." How did Mary instead cling to God Himself?

Book Chapter 9

1. Have you ever had a moment like Kim describes, when you had to decide whether to give up a dream, a job, or some personal status for the good of your family? What was that like? If you

haven't had that experience, imagine what it might be like in your home. What would be major considerations?

2. Think what it meant to Andrew and his business partners when Jesus asked them to give up their careers as fishermen—on the spur of the moment, it seems. What do you imagine their wives and families thought?

3. What must Ruth have had to give up to cling to Naomi and to God? Imagine flying from your home in the United States and landing in Spain, then staying there permanently with your husband's mom. How would you feel in a situation like that?

4. Clinging to God, as Daniel's story reveals, means you let go of some other important things. We don't have enough hands to hold onto God while grasping all the other things that are so enticing. What is the value of clinging to God even if it means letting go of some other good thing?

5. Esther let go of good, but secondary, things. To save her people, she had to risk letting go of what is most precious to all of us: life itself. Yet she clung to God and did the right thing. How does her story challenge you to cling to God no matter what?

Book Chapter 10

1. Kim mentions that while Joshua was clinging to God, he also saw in the people around him "what it looks like not to cling." Do you see that too? How have you seen fellow believers tripped up in their faith by a failure to cling? What results from that?

2. Think about the heavy weight of responsibility that fell on Joshua's shoulders when Moses died. Have you ever been in a spot where deep responsibility weighed you down? How did your relationship with God help lighten the load?

3. Review Joshua 1:9, Deuteronomy 10:20, and Deuteronomy 11:22–23. What did these verses remind Joshua about what God would do, and then what he should do in relation to God?

4. Recall how Hezekiah placed the letter from Assyria's king before God and prayed over it. What do *you* need to place before God? How will doing that demonstrate "clinging" to the Lord?

5. Kim clarifies that "clinging to God is not a formula we follow so that we get whatever we want"—to cling to God is to acknowledge our love for Him, our desire to follow Him, and the fact that our Savior deserves our loyalty. But in clinging, *we* benefit. What are some of the ways clinging relentlessly to God can affect our lives?